# Oklahoma Route 66

# Oklahoma
# Route 66
### SECOND EDITION

## Jim Ross

SECOND EDITION (2ND PRINTING)

OKLAHOMA ROUTE 66
Copyright © 2011 by Jim Ross

GHOST TOWN PRESS
13100 E. Old Highway 66
Arcadia, Oklahoma 73007-7909

Printed in China through Four Colour Print Group, Louisville, KY

The author thanks Arthur Krim for permission to quote from his article, "Mapping Route 66: A Cultural Cartography," published in *Roadside America*, University of Iowa Press, 1990.

Maps
Unless otherwise credited, all maps were created by and are copyrighted by Jim Ross.

Cover Art / Design
Shellee Graham

Book Design / Layout
Jim Ross and Shellee Graham

Photos
All photographs are by the author unless otherwise credited.

Front Cover and Page Opposite
State Line Station (ca. 1930s) - courtesy Oklahoma Department of Transportation.

Half Title Page
Model A Fords in Chandler © 2010 Jerry McClanahan

Title Page
1950s Traffic West of Arcadia - courtesy Oklahoma Department of Transportation

Back Cover
Oklahoma City Corvette Club west of Weatherford © 1993 Jerry McClanahan

ISBN: 978-0-9677481-7-7

*Snapshot in Time:*
*Oklahoma Route 66 at the Kansas state line in 1949,*
*looking toward Baxter Springs, Kansas.*

*Oklahoma Department of Transportation*

*The neon sign at Sapulpa's OK Motel, now gone, was one of those soft beacons in the night meant to catch the eye of weary travelers.*
*Shellee Graham*

*To the keepers of the highway*

*and*

*To my Dad, for those*
*unforgettable two-lane vacations*

*1940s traffic on Southwest Blvd. (US 66) in Red Fork, then a Tulsa suburb.*
Oklahoma Department of Transportation

# Table of Contents

*Built in 1917 by the Rochester Bridge Co. of Rochester, Indiana, this steel truss bridge on Dosie Creek east of Davenport, Oklahoma, was one of the oldest existing Route 66 bridges still in use when it was demolished in July 2004.*

*The 6-lane paving of Lincoln Blvd. in Oklahoma City is celebrated with a parade in June 1958.*

Oklahoma Department of Transportation

# Acknowledgments

The accuracy of the information in this book is owed chiefly to two individuals: David Lopez (now retired) and Gary Ray Howell of the Oklahoma Department of Transportation. David's knowledge of the road and his ability to quickly locate key documents was truly remarkable. Following his departure, Gary Ray stepped in to aptly fill the void, and to this day he still returns my phone calls without feigned pleasantries. No attempts are made to dissuade me, regardless of how peripheral the request, and inevitably he goes beyond my initial inquiry to provide the most thorough response possible. To them both I express my sincerest gratitude.

A generous thank-you is due also to Michael Wallis, the Mother Road's ambassador emeritus. The publication of Michael's *Route 66, The Mother Road* not only helped launch the renaissance, it steered me onto the path of rediscovery. Early on, Michael and wife Suzanne graciously took me under their wing (yes, they are as one), and taught me ways of navigating the world of 66 I could have learned nowhere else.

My old research partner, Jerry McClanahan, more than anyone is responsible for fueling my insatiable "need to know" regarding the evolution of the highway. Unsurpassed as a Route 66 artist or investigator, his primary research in the days when the route was still the route establishes him as a true pioneer in recording the cartographic history of US 66.

I must express my appreciation as well to Mother Road advocates Kathy Anderson and Carol Duncan, both of whom have been reliable resources since my first guidebook, the rudimentary *Cruiser's Companion*, made its debut almost twenty years ago. The same recognition goes to my friend Frank Maloney, explorer of both galaxies and old roads, who first introduced me to the world of aerial imagery and who still makes it his business to raise the questions no one else asks.

Others who contributed directly or provided valuable input include artist and photographer Shellee Graham, historian Arthur Krim, and the late Vivian Payne, widow of Bunion Derby winner Andy Payne. To these and all the others who have offered encouragement and support over the years, a warm and hearty salute!

# Foreword by Jerry McClanahan

     I first became acquainted with Jim Ross through his earlier book, *The Cruiser's Companion*, published way back in 1992. Not having had the pleasure of knowing Mr. Ross, I wondered what the heck this guy could know about Oklahoma's Route 66 that I didn't.

     Quite a lot, as it turned out.

     This was driven home with the first edition of his "magnum okie," (er, make that opus), *Oklahoma Route 66*, for which I had the honor of designing the cover.

     Jim knows more about US 66 through the 46th state than would be healthy for anyone with less fervor for historic accuracy. No matter how hard I try to come up with some fact about the Oklahoma road that Jim missed or goofed up, I am foiled at every turn of the old Portland Concrete. Jim has firmly cemented the path of 66 through decades of evolution. Suffice it to say that *Oklahoma Route 66* has proven to be a trustworthy and fascinating record of history's most famous highway through one of the Route's most historic states.

     Oklahoma's importance is undeniable. Not only does the red-dirt state keep Kansas and Texas from bumping into each other, it anchors the route smack in the middle of the American heartland. As

Michael Wallis, famed author and the voice of the Sheriff in *CARS*, pointed out in his intro to this book's first edition, "without Oklahoma's almost 400 miles of vintage roadway, there would never have been a Route 66." He got that right. As related in this very book, it was "good roads" booster Cyrus Avery of Tulsa who was responsible for the route being christened with those famous "twin sixes" of lore.

As history attests, US 66 first gained the world's attention with the cross-country "Bunion Derby" footrace of 1928, won by Foyil, Oklahoma, native Andy Payne. Another grueling race, this time against hunger and poverty, ensued in the next decade. Steinbeck's *The Grapes of Wrath* chronicled the fortitude of farm families fleeing hard times down the "Mother Road," thousands of dust bowl Okies lured by the "promised land" waiting at the end of Route 66. After World War II, when prosperity had finally found its way back to the highway and the troops were home, bristling with a newfound wanderlust needing expression, Route 66 ferried hordes of vacationers to the grand sights of the American West.

For many Easterners, the state of Oklahoma was where they first encountered the roadside west of cowboys and Indians, buffalo and wild mustangs. Today, tourists from all over the world remain eager to set tires upon the hallowed pavement through the Sooner State, and dedicated researchers and preservationists, like Jim, still work to save as much of our route's history as possible, striving to ensure that there will always be a Route 66 for everyone to enjoy.

Over eight decades after the birth of US 66, the old road is cracked and worn, and memories are fading as fast as leaves falling on an abandoned stretch of old pavement. Thanks to Jim, however, we have an indelible record of the places and faces and remaining traces of what makes Route 66 the Main Street of America and Oklahoma its native state. Hit this book, and then hit the road. You'll be richer for the experience.

Jerry McClanahan
Chandler, Oklahoma

# Preface

A little over a decade ago, I published the first edition of this book. It was a long process, particularly for one with limited computer graphics skills. The maps alone took twelve months to complete. Only then was the first word written. It was a time during which I was often asked the question, "When will the book be out?" My answer, admittedly evasive, borrowed from a slogan belonging to one of the road's enduring icons. "It's worth waiting for," I would chime.

In the preface I followed that up with the comment that to be worth waiting for, a book must contain something of value and fulfill a promise to its intended audience. As it was then, it is my goal now to deliver on both counts.

This new edition of *Oklahoma Route 66*, like the first, serves a number of purposes. Foremost, it is a hands-on guide for casual tourists as well as those who yearn to explore the road in Oklahoma to the greatest extent possible. It is also meant to provide a record of the highway's physical evolution from its inception in 1926 through its decertification in 1985 and beyond. Only slight emphasis has been placed on Route 66 personalities and the historical landmarks that decorate the roadside (subjects well covered in other publications), though some are represented, either in pictures or in the text.

First released in 2001, *Oklahoma Route 66* quickly became recognized as the most comprehensive accounting of a segment of the route yet published. This was due almost entirely to its focus and resulted, simply enough, from the sheer volume of accumulated documentation. This new edition remains loyal to its predecessor. Maps were updated to reflect alterations in the route. While layout and text are fundamentally unchanged, the jacket was redesigned and many of the first edition photos have been replaced. The biggest improvement, by far, is converting to full color, which is nice for the photos, but especially helpful with the maps.

Although the following represents years of research, there are still limits to what can be said with certainty in terms of the highway's original or subsequent pathways. It is one thing to locate and chart surviving roadbed that is adequately documented. Establishing alignments with scant, if any, records to support their existence is another matter. In those instances, I relied on what I have learned about preferred road building practices and protocols used by the Oklahoma Department of Transportation.

On a more personal note, I am sometimes asked what Route 66 means to me. Inevitably I find myself searching for words or offering a quick, canned response. After all, I didn't grow up on old 66. My own connection is rooted more in glorified memories of 2-lane family vacations in the 1950s and the television show *route 66* than in youthful encounters with the Mother Road. Oftentimes I simply reply that it is the call of the open road and the opportunity for adventure that call embodies. Added to that, I conclude, is the chance to share experiences with valued friends and to make new acquaintances along the way.

The sentimental part of me would not stop there, however. A more soulful, contemplative response would tell a tale of communion, one that occurs in quiet moments—usually at dusk—and takes place strictly between myself and the expanse of highway before me. It is then that the spirits of the road sometimes permit me to feel their fleeting embrace and with it the collective power of every story ever recorded by the silent, sturdy roadway.

Perhaps a more accurate way to answer that question would be to say that, with Route 66, I feel a sense of *place*. That is a comfortable fit for me. I suspect the same could be said, to some level, of most 66ers, be they tourists, explorers, wanderers, or dreamers. That is what makes the lure irresistible for so many and what makes the Route 66 community a family in the truest sense.

Travel safe. Savor the journey. Feel the power.

Jim Ross
Arcadia, Oklahoma

*Sunset at Pops, Arcadia*

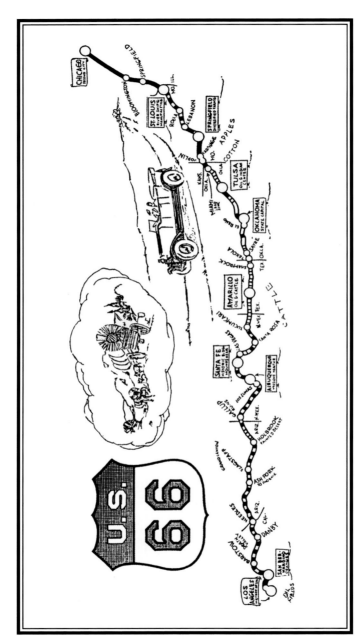

*Early map of Route 66, published by* American Motorist *in 1927. Author's collection*

# Past, Present & Future

While November 11, 1926, is universally accepted as the day US 66 drew first breath, technically that is the day the new numbering system for all US routes was formally adopted by the American Association of State Highway Officials (AASHO) for the new network of national highways. And though numbers already had been assigned to specific roadways or linkages of roads, signifying their "birth," approval by individual states was required before the new federal routes could officially become part of their own highway systems. In Oklahoma, approval came from State Highway Commission action on December 7, 1926, which likely was their first scheduled meeting following the November 11th AASHO ceremony.

The pathway chosen for 66—state roads 39, 7, and 3—roughly followed one branch of the former Ozark Trails (in eastern Oklahoma) as well as the railroad, and in places overlapped the existing Postal Route. At the time, these state highways were mostly unimproved, especially in rural areas, so it became a priority for all concerned to get Route 66 paved, border to border.

At the head of this effort was Cyrus S. Avery, who in 1927 became president of the newly founded National US Highway 66 Association. His involvement with the Ozark Trails Association ten years earlier and his chairmanship of the Oklahoma State Highway Commission from 1923-1926 had established him as a leader in the development of better roads. Only a year before, it was Avery who had been the driving force behind the creation of the route destined to become the world's most famous highway, and who would later become known as the Father of Route 66.

1

It was in 1924, during his days as Oklahoma State Highway Commissioner, that Avery was chosen by US Agriculture Secretary Howard Gore to serve on a joint board with other state highway officials in the creation of a whole new system of interstate roads. He was also selected to head a committee within that board to develop a uniform marking system for the proposed new federal routes.

F.J. Gentry
MEMBER

Roy M. Johnson
VICE CHAIRMAN

Cyrus S. Avery
CHAIRMAN

E. Bee Guthrey
SECRETARY

J.M Page
STATE HIGHWAY ENGINEER

*Oklahoma*
State Highway Commission
January 1, 1927

*Oklahoma Department of Transportation*

The board's work was completed near the end of 1925. Avery, with assistance from officials B.H. Piepmeier of Missouri and Frank Sheets of Illinois, had been successful in ensuring that one of the major routes—Chicago to Los Angeles—would cross Oklahoma end to end, even though it had been the subject of considerable debate over charges that it catered to the interests of its creators. The committee had by then also received from the US Bureau of Public

Roads approval on the numbering system that would be applied nationwide.

Because of its importance among the routes as a whole, the number 60—prominent within the numbering scheme—had been assigned to Avery's road. But this choice came under attack from the governor of Kentucky, William Fields, who felt insulted with the assignment of the subordinate number 62 for his state's east-west route, which he argued should link with the Chicago-Los Angeles road at Springfield, Missouri to create a true trans-coastal highway.

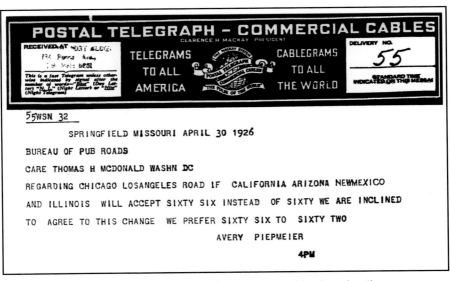

*The "Springfield Telegram," which resulted in changing the*
*number of the Chicago-to-Los Angeles route from US 60 to US 66.*
National Archives (provided by Richard Weingroff of the Federal Highway Administration)

Avery's camp, in turn, balked at the suggestion of changing designations at such a late date, or worse, breaking up their route, and a stalemate ensued. The controversy was settled only after Avery, desperate to move forward, called for a meeting of his group in Springfield, Missouri, on April 30, 1926. It was an election year in Oklahoma, and should the incumbent governor lose his job, as predicted, Avery was sure to lose his as well.

It was during this meeting, in evaluating available numbers, that Oklahoma Chief Engineer John M. Page suggested the number 66, as it had not been assigned. After some discussion, it was agreed, and a telegram signed by Avery and Missouri's Piepmeier was sent that afternoon to Bureau of Public Roads chief Thomas H. McDonald in Washington, D.C. For Missouri, it meant destroying maps already published with Route 66 depicted as US 60, and while the number 66 was less prestigious than 60, it was preferred over the rejected number 62.

In November, Martin Trapp was voted out as Oklahoma's governor, and Cyrus Avery prepared to leave public service. He did not, however, retire. By the spring of 1927 he was in the forefront to get Route 66 paved as head of the new National US Highway 66 Association.

A. L. Commons of Miami, secretary-member of the State Highway commission, holding giant scissors which will be used in ribbon-cutting ceremony Sept. 13 marking the official opening of the new Miami-Afton pavement on U. S. Highway 66, the Will Rogers highway, to traffic. Photograph was taken at east end of new bridge over the Neosho river, where ceremonies will be held.

*From the Miami News-Record, September 5, 1937,*
*under the headline: "Giant Scissors Ready for Road*
*Opening Ceremony." Used with permission*

Paving occurred piecemeal as funds became available, and required eleven years to complete. It was a concerted effort involving not only the association's push, but cooperation among various governmental jurisdictions and even adjoining states, who were equally eager to eliminate areas of difficult passage and attract motorists. The last stretch to be uniformly paved was completed in 1937 when the existing road between Miami and Afton, which had been paved nine feet wide in 1922, was bypassed. The closing of this final gap was celebrated in grand style at the new bridge over the Neosho River in Miami on September 13th of that year, drawing dignitaries and spectators from around the state.

Promotion of the highway was also a top priority for the national association, and during those early years recognition of the highway grew steadily as a result of widely distributed literature that beckoned America to find its way west on Route 66. Yet in spite of the enthusiasm generated by the Association and public officials, 1930s America struggled in the wake of the stock market crash and

*Highway booster club from El Reno, 1932.*
Oklahoma Department of Transportation

the punishing drought that drove thousands of families from ruined land in Oklahoma and surrounding states.

On Route 66, paving progressed in spite of the hard times, and traffic counts were on the rise, though due in some measure to the plight of migrant families in search of deliverance. As a result, business on the highway became brisk, if not profitable, and the Association busied itself soliciting more members.

Franklin Roosevelt's New Deal gradually got Americans working again, and the coming of World War II mobilized the country. At war's end, a sense of elation and new beginnings swept the land. The first book about the route, *A Guide Book to Highway 66*, was published in 1946 by Jack Rittenhouse, the same year the song destined to become the highway's anthem, *Route 66*, was written by Bobby Troup. 1946 was also the year a barber from Clinton, Jack Cutberth, signed on as Secretary of the Association's Oklahoma chapter, a job that later earned him the position of National Executive Secretary and the title "Mr. 66."

*"Mr. 66," Jack Cutberth with wife Gladys, ca. 1970s.*

*Courtesy Gladys Cutberth*

Operating out of a basement office in their Clinton home, Jack and wife Gladys spent more than two decades traveling and promoting Route 66, an effort that contributed greatly to the highway's prominence and, ultimately, its legend.

The baby boom was well under way by the late 1940s, and as the 1950s rolled around more and more families were in the mood to travel. Cars were flashier, bigger, and faster than ever, and on the open road there awaited a legion of hosts to serve their every need. As traffic increased, so did competition for tourist dollars, and the result was a roadside soon littered with billboards, motels, filling stations, curio shops, and diners, many of them drenched in throbbing neon.

It was a prosperous and fun time for the keepers of the highway and motorists alike, yet the end had already been foretold. Military truck convoys during the war had exacted a heavy price on a roadway built for lighter loads, and traffic had reached levels that were no longer acceptable in terms of safety and convenience. Four-lane projects were on the increase and, as the 1950s came to a close, construction of the new limited access interstate highway system was gaining steam.

During the 1960s, Route 66 was methodically dismantled and reconfigured. Many sections were either abandoned or consumed by the super slab, while others became access roads or were turned over to local jurisdictions to do with as they saw fit. Towns were bypassed and long stretches of road became isolated. By the mid-1970s, America's Main Street had all but vanished, and in 1985, the last of the signs came down when it was officially decertified as a federal route. Some states chose to redesignate parts of it as a state highway; otherwise, Route 66 disappeared from road maps completely.

Yet almost on the heels of its official demise, the resurrection began, and many remaining business owners—those stalwart survivors who had refused to quit—found new life. By the end of the

*Westbound motorists between Arcadia and Edmond, ca. 1953.*
*Oklahoma Department of Transportation*

1980s, state associations had been formed, preservationists were at work, and traffic was picking up. By its 75th Anniversary, the Mother Road had become a focal point for historians, photographers, media moguls, revivalists, and good old-fashioned vacationers from coast to coast and around the world.

Critics called it a phase that wouldn't last; enthusiasts and those who understood the road's historic value ignored them. By the end of the 20th Century, countless books, magazines, videos, works of art, documentaries, and commemorative souvenirs of every imaginable type had found their way into homes worldwide, and the flow of motorists exploring and learning about Route 66 continued to thicken.

*Dash plaque from the 1st Oklahoma*
*Route 66 Association Cruise.*
*Author's collection*

There has been no let up and no looking back. For Mother Road shopkeepers, both seasoned and up-and-coming, the future looks bright.

If, and when, it levels off will likely be decided by a future generation. Geographer Arthur Krim suggests that, "Route 66 has become an icon of the auto age because it encompassed both the real geography of westward migration and the abstract need to symbolize the independence of the American road." His assessment offers insight into the strength of the highway's appeal and, perhaps more importantly, why its influence continues to be felt by millions.

Due to the efforts of preservation organizations and the support of historical societies and other advocates, its memory, at least, is assured. Museums dedicated to Route 66, the ever-expanding archive of literature devoted to the road, landmarks that have become recognized historical sites, and hundreds of miles of road still sporting those rhythmic sixes as state highways guarantee it.

Route 66. It is many things to many people—an adventure, an escape, a memory re-lived, a destination in itself. It helped shape the country's cultural evolution in the 20th Century and left an indelible mark on the American landscape. It is history, it is people, it is a story of both struggle and triumph and, most of all, it is undying.

And so the legend grows.

*Just in the last ten years, several vintage stations like this one in Davenport have been rescued and either restored or preserved.*
*Shellee Graham*

# The
# Road

"A highway is never finished. There is always something that can be done to make it better, safer and of greater utility."

*—From the Oklahoma Highway Commission's 1928 Annual Report*

OFFICIAL LIFE SPAN OF US 66 IN OKLAHOMA

December 7, 1926 — April 1, 1985

OFFICIAL HISTORIC ROUTING OF US 66 IN OKLAHOMA

From the Minutes of the State Highway Commission meeting on the above date in 1926:

"The Joint Board of Interstate Highways, appointed by the U.S. Secretary of Agriculture on February 20th, 1925, . . . has completed its work and selected certain routes of the Oklahoma State Highway system to be included in the Federal System.

"U.S. Route 66. Beginning at a point on the Kansas state line south of Baxter Springs, follows State Route 39 to the junction with State Highway No. 7 at the town of Commerce, thence follows Route 7 through Miami, Vinita, Tulsa, Chandler, Oklahoma City, thence follows State Highway No. 3 to El Reno, Bridgeport, Clinton, [and] Sayre to the Texas State line near Texola."

## OKLAHOMA ROUTE 66 IN MILES

ESTIMATED MILEAGE
### 1926 Historic Alignment — 415.4 miles

FROM OKLAHOMA DEPARTMENT OF TRANSPORTATION RECORDS
### 1936 — 383.7 miles
(Of this, 371.6 miles was paved and 12.1 miles was untreated gravel. It is probable that the first paved alignment completed in 1937 matches the 1936 total.)

### 1944 — 381.7 miles
### 1951 — 368.0 miles

## COMPLETION OF FIRST-GENERATION PAVING
### 1937

## ROAD SURFACES IN OKLAHOMA — to 1937

Graded Earth
Gravel (also known as TBSC, or Traffic Bound Surface Course)

Oiled Gravel
Brick
Macadam (thin, rudimentary paving consisting of crushed
          stone mixed with tar or asphalt)
Asphalt (including rock, sheet, and single bituminous)
Asphalt over a concrete base with concrete edges
Portland Concrete

    The variety of surfaces used is explained in the commission's annual report for 1924. "The choice has generally depended upon the funds available and the recommendations of the state highway engineer regarding traffic conditions probable in the near future, the sub-grade conditions, the materials available, etc."
    Surfaces of choice to uniformly pave Route 66 were Portland Concrete and asphalt over a concrete base and, except for a few miles surfaced with brick or pure asphalt, these two types accounted for virtually its entire length, with Portland Concrete most prevalent.

10

## PAVING STANDARDS

Prior to 1923, standards varied. Some existing pavement, such as the road between Miami and Afton (paved in 1922), was as narrow as nine feet.

1924 — Standard rights-of-way were set at 66 feet, though existing roadway widths still varied.

1925 — Minimum roadway widths set at 18 feet with 80-foot rights-of-way.

1930 — Minimum roadway widths increased to 20 feet with 100-foot rights-of-way.

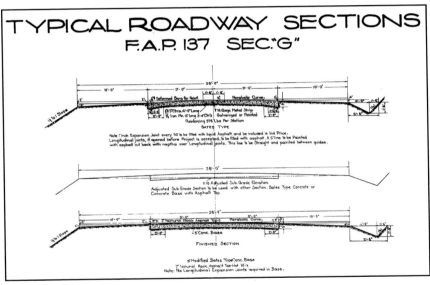

*Design specifications for a 1928 Route 66 paving project east of Arcadia.*
*Oklahoma Department of Transportation*

## IMPROVEMENTS

Improvements to the state's highways were already underway at the time Route 66 was dedicated late in 1926. In the commission's annual report for that year, an introduction prepared by Cyrus Avery's chief engineer J. M. Page stated that: "We have four survey parties continuously at work and are pushing vigorously the work of properly locating the State Highway system. Many miles of distance between controlling points have been eliminated by careful location uninfluenced by the circuitous or section line location of the present

*Early road grading equipment.*
Oklahoma Department of Transportation

roads." He also noted that, "Many unnecessary railroad grade crossings have been eliminated, square turns and short curves done away with."

Whether or not to modernize the highway department with road building machinery was addressed in the same report by Avery himself — " . . the question that confronted the Commission was whether we would motorize the department or whether we would adopt the individual patrol system of the one-man, horse or mule blade grader." It was decided that for at least the year 1927, funds would be better spent on labor supplied by the individual patrolman, who provided all of his own equipment.

Having adopted the new interstate system of marking its highways, the commission reported that, "We expect in the next sixty days to have every state highway so carefully marked through the country and through the cities, that all that will be necessary is to know the number of the route that takes you to your point of destination."

Though safety has always been a consideration, eliminating the dangers caused by poor road surfaces or perilous turns and railroad crossings seemed the focus in the early years. It wasn't until 1929 that the commission reported attempts undertaken to protect motorists from each other. "By the adoption of the modern system of center lining all paved highways, the marking of hills and dangerous curves with a white line, and the installation of proper signs warning the public not to cross these white lines, a greater degree of safety has been attained."

A curious oddity of early paving involved the sloping curbs on some stretches of Portland Concrete, particularly in Western Oklahoma. The curbs were used in hilly areas as a way to keep water on the road until it could be discharged through gutters placed at strategic points, thus preventing rapid erosion of the soft shoulders. While they served their purpose, the curbs soon proved to be hazardous to motorists, as they created the potential for hydroplaning during heavy rains and could cause drivers to lose control when unintentionally running up on them.

Over time, much of the first paved route was improved with hard shoulders, resurfaced, or realigned, and the curbs were eliminated. Notably, several long stretches of original and unaltered PC paving remain in western Oklahoma, complete with curbs and gutters (see photo on page 138). Today, these sections are used only for local traffic.

*This 1939 WPA-built bridge is south of Erick on the 1926-1928 alignment, which followed the old postal route.*

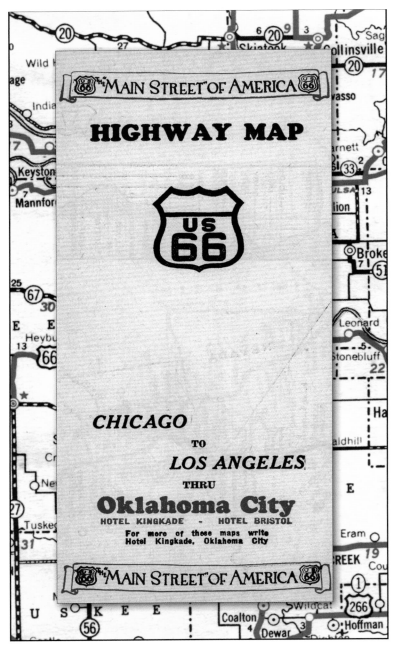

*Free maps like this one were widely distributed by the US 66 Association.*
Author's collection

# About the Maps

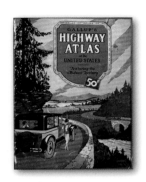

US 66 in Oklahoma, as elsewhere, is today a complicated arrangement of intertwining and sometimes discontinuous roadways, many of which are unmarked. The maps in this book were designed to identify those roadways, beginning with the first, or historic, route in 1926. They are based on archival documents, a variety of vintage maps, and other source material compiled over two decades and corroborated through extensive field research and innumerable consultations with transportation officials and other historians.

With any such effort, errors are a virtual certainty, either due to something overlooked or evidence not yet discovered, and while earnest attempts were made to verify each pathway depicted, in a few instances judgment calls were required.

With this in mind, the history of Route 66 can best be thought of in three phases:

- The historic, or first alignment, parts of which were discarded as the route was uniformly paved.
- The first paved alignment and subsequent changes to that routing.
- The 4-lane/interstate alignments in the western part of the state.

The maps reflect all three eras, and were designed to serve a dual purpose: to partner with the driving directions and to provide historical details on the highway's evolution. While they may appear complex, they were assembled in a way that allows you to use only the parts you need. The driving directions allow for ease of navigation, regardless of the extent one chooses to explore. For those who want to understand the sequence of events behind each change, that information is included as well. It should be noted that while temporary alignments are official routes, detours are not, and have not been accounted for.

The following should be kept in mind when using the maps:

- Maps are to scale, however scales vary from one map to the next.
- All maps assume a westbound orientation.
- Route 66 is referred to as "westbound" (W/B) and "eastbound" (E/B), regardless of its true direction at a given point.
- Dashed lines represent sections of road that have been obliterated, are fragmented, or are discontinuous.
- A black bar across a roadway indicates no access or end of road.
- Incidental roads, such as service roads, may be depicted only in part, even though they continue.
- Unverified alignments are characterized as "possible" or "probable," depending on the strength of evidence supporting their inclusion.
- Dates of surfacing shown in the box headed by the "framed" US 66 shield on each map relate only to first-generation paving or the initial paving of a later alignment.
- Sections of the Ozark Trails are identified only where there is interplay with US 66, and are not considered proven alignments.
- Railroads shown may be active or inactive, and were included only where needed or as space allowed.

TERMS
PC = Portland Concrete
First Generation Paving = First Paved Alignment

16

Dates of alignments should be considered approximate. This is due primarily to the lapse between the time plans were first proposed or approved and the time of actual construction. Historically, there is also a gap between "official" completion dates and the dates roadways open for traffic. In a few instances, the absence of records or contradictions among sources required that dates be estimated.

The written driving directions are intended to provide a "through" route, and include only some of the alternative alignments. Bear in mind also that Route 66 is still in use and still changing, so be prepared to make adjustments as you go.

### COLOR CODES

Colors depict successive pathways of the route *on a given map*, and they may not coincide with dates. Facing page maps are treated as one. Expanding a roadway is not treated as a realignment.

GREEN: Original or Historic pathway (whether paved or not)
RED: First realignment to the original roadway
BLUE: Second realignment

Subsequent Upgrades:
ORANGE (Third)
OLIVE GREEN (Fourth)
DARK BROWN (Fifth)

*Road repair at the Classen traffic circle in Oklahoma City, 1957. Note the smudge pots in front of the barricade.*
Archives & Manuscripts Division, Oklahoma Historical Society

*Afton Station*

# The Tour

"The only objective we, of Oklahoma, have had, was to have a continuous route number from Chicago to Los Angeles without any branches. We assure you that it will be a road through Oklahoma that the U.S. Government will be proud of."

*—Cyrus S. Avery, in a letter dated July 26, 1926 to Design Chief E.W. James of the US Bureau of Public Roads*

*Looking toward Baxter Springs, Kansas at the state line, 1949.*
*Oklahoma Department of Transportation*

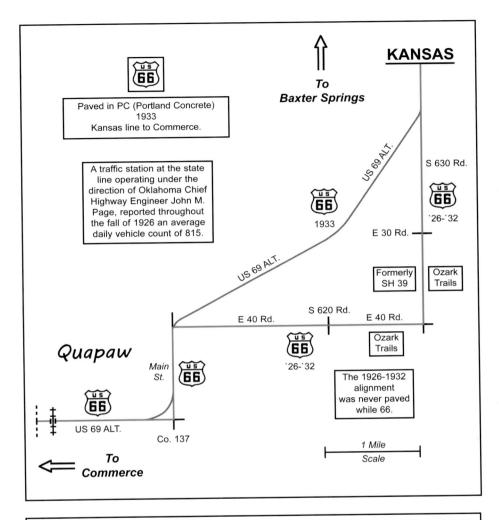

US 66

Paved in PC (Portland Concrete)
1933
Kansas line to Commerce.

KANSAS

To
Baxter Springs

A traffic station at the state line operating under the direction of Oklahoma Chief Highway Engineer John M. Page, reported throughout the fall of 1926 an average daily vehicle count of 815.

US 69 ALT.

US 66
1933

S 630 Rd.

US 66
'26-'32

E 30 Rd.

US 69 ALT.

Formerly
SH 39

Ozark
Trails

S 620 Rd.

E 40 Rd.

E 40 Rd.

Ozark
Trails

Quapaw

Main
St.

US 66

US 66
'26-'32

The 1926-1932 alignment was never paved while 66.

US 66

US 69 ALT.

Co. 137

1 Mile
Scale

To
Commerce

FROM THE KANSAS STATE LINE, HEAD SOUTH ON US 69 ALT. THROUGH **QUAPAW**, CURVING TO THE RIGHT AT THE SOUTH END OF TOWN.

Located on a site once occupied by the Quapaw Indians less than five miles from the Kansas line, Quapaw is the easternmost town on Oklahoma Route 66. Cattle and hay were primary early resources, but it was the mining of zinc, begun around 1897, and specifically the ore churned out of the Dark Horse Mine in the early 1900s that became the town's mainstay.

Today, reminders of the boom years can be found along the highway in both directions, where mounds of waste rock called "chat" and associated relics of long-ago mining operations still decorate the

*A wall mural in Quapaw depicts the heyday of mining in northeastern Oklahoma.*

landscape. Colorful murals painted on some of the town's buildings have become a signet of this Route 66 cornerstone.

Down the road, near Tar Creek, lies Commerce, which is probably best known as home to the "Commerce Comet," baseball legend Mickey Mantle. The town began as North Miami, then changed its name to Commerce on June 1, 1914. North Miami didn't die, however, it redeveloped just south of Commerce. Like Quapaw, Commerce has its roots in lead and zinc mining, with the once

*Looking north on Mickey Mantle Blvd. in Commerce, 1952.*

*Oklahoma Department of Transportation*

ENTERING **COMMERCE** ON US 69, TURN RIGHT ON COMMERCE STREET AND LEFT ON MAIN FOR THE HISTORIC ROUTE,
OR,
STAY ON US 69 (MICKEY MANTLE BLVD.) AND CONTINUE TO MIAMI.

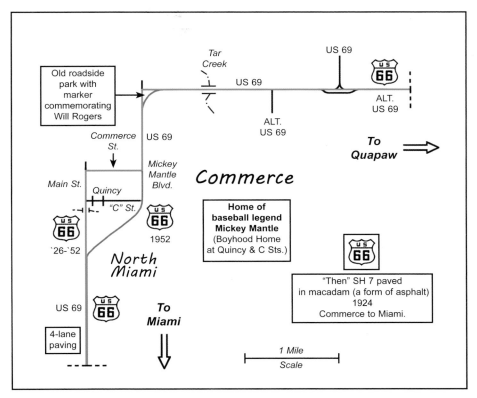

Tar Creek

US 69

US 69

**66** U S

Old roadside park with marker commemorating Will Rogers

ALT. US 69

ALT. US 69

Commerce St.

US 69

Mickey Mantle Blvd.

*Commerce*

**To Quapaw** ⟹

Main St.

Quincy

"C" St.

**66** U S

1952

**66** U S

`26-`52

*North Miami*

**Home of baseball legend Mickey Mantle** (Boyhood Home at Quincy & C Sts.)

**66** U S

US 69

**66** U S

**To Miami**

"Then" SH 7 paved in macadam (a form of asphalt) 1924 Commerce to Miami.

4-lane paving

1 Mile
Scale

*Allen's Conoco in downtown Commerce is a restored architectural gem located on the historic pathway.*

23

prosperous Turkey Fat Mine located right in town. Mickey Mantle's boyhood home, in a modest white-frame house, can be found just off the historic alignment on the northeast corner of "C" and Quincy Streets.

Reportedly, Miami (pronounced My-am-uh), seat of Ottawa County, was originally named Jimtown after four farmers named Jim who lived in the area of present-day North Miami. By 1890 a post office was needed to handle mail destined for the nearby Quapaw Agency, and that was accomplished on April 13, 1891 with help from one of the Jims, that being Jim Palmer, who named the site of the new office "Miami" in honor of his wife's Miami Indian heritage.

In 1905, lead and zinc were discovered, and the rush to excavate the valuable ore resulted in a population boom. In 1919 the Northeastern School of Mines opened on the east side of town, which later became Northeastern Oklahoma A&M College.

Today, Miami's crown jewel is the Coleman Theatre Beautiful, built in Spanish Mission Revival style in 1929 by George L. Coleman, Sr., as a vaudeville and movie theater. In 1989, the theater, suffering from years of neglect, was given to the city by the Coleman family and has since been completely renovated and reopened.

Until recently, Miami was proprietor of another significant landmark, the 1937 steel truss bridge spanning the Neosho River that, when built, completed the final link of Route 66 paving in Oklahoma (see photo on page 4). Because this bridge was mistakenly omitted from a 1993 historic bridge inventory commissioned by the transportation department, it was destroyed after its replacement was completed in 1997, despite a concentrated last minute effort by Route 66 advocates to preserve it.

The original alignment leaving the city is a landmark in its

IN **MIAMI**, TURN RIGHT AT THE INTERSECTION WITH STEVE OWENS BLVD. (JCT. SH 10), CROSS THE NEOSHO RIVER, AND STAY WITH US 69 TO AFTON,
OR,
GO STRAIGHT THROUGH THE INTERSECTION, CROSS THE NEOSHO RIVER ON SOUTH MAIN (THE HISTORIC ALIGNMENT), WHICH BECOMES "E" ST. S.W. PROCEED TO THE T-INTERSECTION, THEN TURN RIGHT FOR 1/4 MILE TO PICK UP THE "SIDEWALK" HIGHWAY AND FOLLOW IT TO A RECONNECTION WITH THE PRIMARY ROUTE (PAGE 29). TURN LEFT THROUGH **NARCISSA**, THEN RIGHT AT THE VO-TECH JUST BEFORE THE I-44 OVERPASS (PAGE 31). CONTINUE ON THE 9-FOOT ROAD TO ITS JUNCTION WITH THE MAIN ROUTE AND TURN RIGHT TO ENTER **AFTON**.

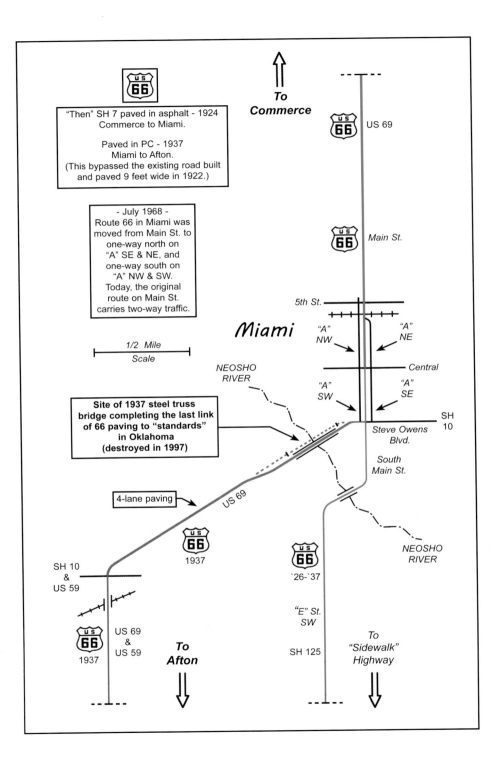

US 66

"Then" SH 7 paved in asphalt - 1924
Commerce to Miami.

Paved in PC - 1937
Miami to Afton.
(This bypassed the existing road built
and paved 9 feet wide in 1922.)

- July 1968 -
Route 66 in Miami was
moved from Main St. to
one-way north on
"A" SE & NE, and
one-way south on
"A" NW & SW.
Today, the original
route on Main St.
carries two-way traffic.

To
Commerce

US 66   US 69

US 66   Main St.

5th St.

Miami

"A"      "A"
NW       NE

Central

NEOSHO
RIVER

"A"      "A"
SW       SE

1/2 Mile
Scale

Site of 1937 steel truss
bridge completing the last link
of 66 paving to "standards"
in Oklahoma
(destroyed in 1997)

SH
10

Steve Owens
Blvd.

South
Main St.

4-lane paving

US 69

NEOSHO
RIVER

US 66
1937

US 66
`26-`37

SH 10
&
US 59

"E" St.
SW

US 66
1937

US 69
&
US 59

To
Afton

SH 125

To
"Sidewalk"
Highway

*After extensive renovation, the Coleman Theater's neon once again lights up the night.*

*This bridge once spanned the Neosho River at Miami on the original South Main Street alignment, which led to the "Sidewalk Highway."*

Oklahoma Department of Transportation

*1950s postcard view of Miami's Main Street.*

Chief Cards Oklahoma City

own right. Built in 1922 by the Oklahoma Department of Highways, four years before it became part of America's Main Street, this unique and fragile stretch of road linking Miami with Afton was paved only 9 feet wide, including its concrete edges. It is a road remnant unlike any other, and while in spots it is periodically over-laid with gravel, the two surviving sections, together totaling over six miles, can still be driven with care.

*State Highway map depicting the early route of US 66 in northeastern Oklahoma.*
*Oklahoma Department of Transportation*

Though narrow, the "sidewalk" highway was well constructed. Following the same specifications as some of its wider counterparts, it consisted of concrete five inches thick

*Miami's Coleman Theatre Beautiful,*
*built in 1929.*

with nine-inch-wide edges elevated two inches. A layer of asphalt brought the surface flush with the concrete edges. Given the traffic count and speed of cars in 1922, such a narrow highway was not considered unusual. By the mid-1930s, however, the needs of the motoring public had changed dramatically, and this classic strip of America's Main Street was bypassed by the current alignment.

Narcissa, named by early-day settler Narcissa Walker, was established around 1902. It has the distinction of being the only

*The "sidewalk" highway, between Miami and Afton.*

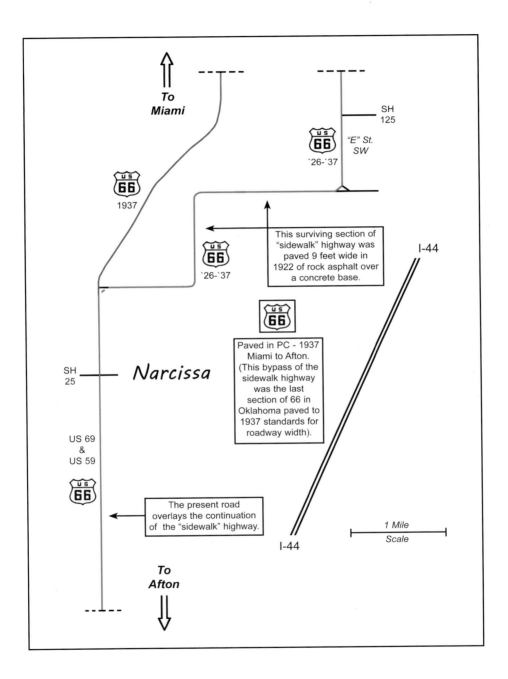

To
Miami

SH
125

US 66
"E" St.
SW
'26-'37

US 66
1937

This surviving section of
"sidewalk" highway was
paved 9 feet wide in
1922 of rock asphalt over
a concrete base.

I-44

US 66
'26-'37

US 66

Paved in PC - 1937
Miami to Afton.
(This bypass of the
sidewalk highway
was the last
section of 66 in
Oklahoma paved to
1937 standards for
roadway width).

SH
25

*Narcissa*

US 69
&
US 59

US 66

The present road
overlays the continuation
of the "sidewalk" highway.

1 Mile
Scale

I-44

To
Afton

town to exist on the path of the 9-foot road, and though there are presently no operating businesses here, patrolling dogs and a few residents remain.

One of the highway's better known and memorable roadside stops was the Buffalo Ranch, just outside Afton at the junction with US 59. Opened by Aleene and Russell Kay in 1953, it contained an array of wildlife, including "the world's only trained buffalo." The Ranch also included a western store and an eatery called The Dairy

*Afton's Buffalo Ranch in the 1950s, featuring the world's only trained buffalo.*
*Gibson Studio, Grove, OK. Jerry McClanahan collection*

Ranch. Buffalo Ranch closed in 1997 with the death of Aleene Kay Albro. A modern truck stop now consumes the site.

Afton, established in 1886 as a farming community along the fertile banks of Horse Creek, was named by railroad surveyor Anton Aires for his daughter, whose namesake was the river Afton in her father's native Scotland, a waterway made famous by a Robert Burns poem.

The existing bridge on Horse Creek was built in 1929 as a replacement to an earlier span, remnants of which can still be found in the creek bed nearby. Its design included a pedestrian walkway on each side, a safety feature not seen on many Route 66 bridges. How long before this classic structure meets the fate of the Neosho

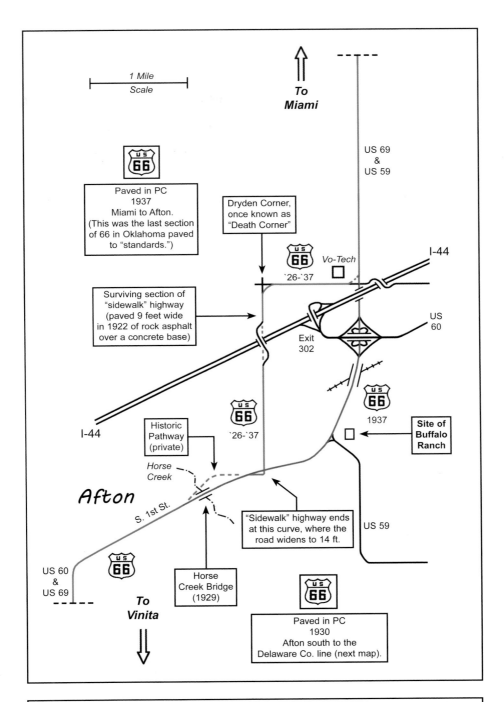

1 Mile
Scale

To
**Miami**

US 69
&
US 59

US 66
Paved in PC
1937
Miami to Afton.
(This was the last section
of 66 in Oklahoma paved
to "standards.")

Dryden Corner,
once known as
"Death Corner"

US 66
`26-`37

Vo-Tech

I-44

Surviving section of
"sidewalk" highway
(paved 9 feet wide
in 1922 of rock asphalt
over a concrete base)

Exit
302

US
60

I-44

US 66
`26-`37

Historic
Pathway
(private)

US 66
1937

Site of
**Buffalo
Ranch**

Horse
Creek

*Afton*

S. 1st St.

"Sidewalk" highway ends
at this curve, where the
road widens to 14 ft.

US 59

US 60
&
US 69

US 66

Horse
Creek Bridge
(1929)

US 66
Paved in PC
1930
Afton south to the
Delaware Co. line (next map).

To
*Vinita*

LEAVING AFTON, FOLLOW US 60 & US 69 SOUTH, THEN CURVE AROUND DEAD MAN'S
CORNER (NEXT MAP) AND HEAD WEST TOWARD VINITA.

*Right:*
*The Dairy Ranch, now gone, was once part of the Buffalo Ranch complex.*

*Center:*
*"Afton Station" was a derelict building until it was restored by Laurel Kane as a visitor's center. Attached is David Kane's Packard Museum.*

*Afton's 1929 Horse Creek Bridge was built with a pedestrian walkway on each side.*

*Left:*
*Afton traffic, late 1950s.*
*Laurel Kane collection*

*Right:*
*Afton traffic 60 years later.*
*Note the missing stop light.*

River Bridge is unknown, but considering the age of most surviving historic Route 66 bridges, there are no guarantees. No doubt, many will soon fall in the absence of repair dollars or preservation efforts.

Afton is well represented with historic architecture such as the ruins of the Rest Haven and Avon motor courts, the Palmer Hotel, and, most notably, a renovated former DX-turned-visitor-center now known as Afton Station. Here, motorists will find a place to stretch,

*Postcard by MWM, Aurora, MO.*
*Author's collection*

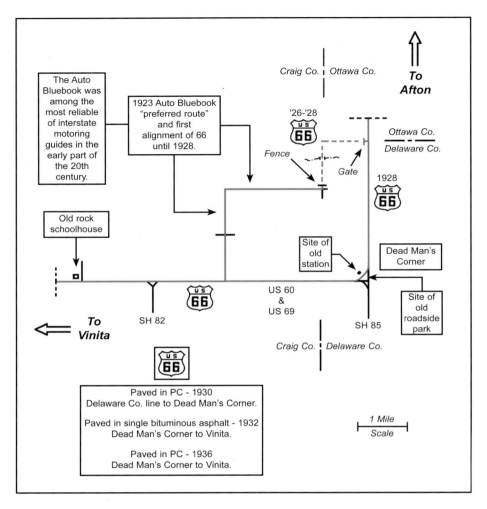

The Auto Bluebook was among the most reliable of interstate motoring guides in the early part of the 20th century.

1923 Auto Bluebook "preferred route" and first alignment of 66 until 1928.

Craig Co. | Ottawa Co.

**To Afton**

'26-'28

US 66

Fence

Gate

Ottawa Co.

Delaware Co.

1928

US 66

Old rock schoolhouse

Site of old station

Dead Man's Corner

US 66

SH 82

US 60 & US 69

Site of old roadside park

**To Vinita**

SH 85

Craig Co. | Delaware Co.

US 66

Paved in PC - 1930
Delaware Co. line to Dead Man's Corner.

Paved in single bituminous asphalt - 1932
Dead Man's Corner to Vinita.

Paved in PC - 1936
Dead Man's Corner to Vinita.

1 Mile
Scale

have a snack, and browse memorabilia-filled display cases. A collection of pristine vintage Packards is housed on-site as well.

Beyond Afton a few miles, Route 66 changes directions from due south to due west at a turn formerly known as Dead Man's Corner, so named because of the hazard it once presented to motorists. This is also the site of a vintage station as well as an old roadside camp, which was a natural fit for the space created when the corner was cropped by the sweeping arc of roadway that still carries traffic today. Until a few years ago, scattered across this time-worn wayside camp were the fragmented ruins of crumbling brick fire pits. Now gone, the warmth they provided in the early years no doubt created life-long memories for those weary travellers who could ill afford the luxury of the motor courts in Vinita or Claremore.

About a mile past the turnoff for SH 82, there is a small building on the right that once was a school, according to a county map from the early 1930s. And at the first section line road west of the Little Cabin Creek Bridge, the early, unpaved alignment swung to the left, onto what is now private property and across a small box drain date-stamped in 1926 by the State Highway Commission. This early alignment reconnects where the present road curves right toward Vinita, as depicted on the map on page 36.

Vinita, home to the Eastern Oklahoma State Hospital and the Eastern Trails Museum, is the seat of Craig County and, like Afton, it is congested with architectural relics attesting to the glory years of

*When the Lewis Motel sign came down and the rest of the complex destroyed, Vinita lost one of its most recognizable icons.*

Route 66. Originally called Downingville, Vinita was re-named in 1871 when two railroads entered the area, the Missouri-Kansas-Topeka and the Atlantic & Pacific. The town's primary promoter, Colonel Elias C. Boudinot, was a Cherokee Indian whose father had earned notoriety from his involvement in selling tribal lands to the US Government, an act that ultimately led to the Trail of Tears migration. Boudinot named the town Vinita in honor of artist Vinnie Ream (1850-1914), whose sculptures include a statue of Abraham Lincoln displayed at the Capitol in Washington, D.C.

*Jim's Restaurant 1/2 mile south of Vinita, ca. 1950.*
Smith's Studio, Vinita, OK. Author's collection

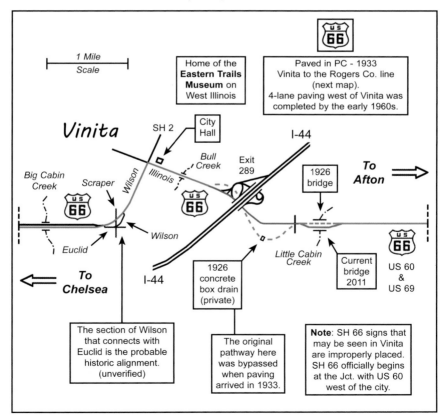

*Vinita in the 1950s. Wright's Cafeteria is on the right.*

*Baxtone, Amarillo, TX*

Leaving Vinita, Route 66 becomes a 4-lane highway. West of town, a couple miles past Big Cabin Creek, US 69 turns off to the south. About a mile farther on, US 60 angles off to the northwest. At that point, the Mother Road becomes SH 66, and remains so all the way to Tulsa.

ENTER **VINITA** ON ILLINOIS. AT WILSON (JCT SH 2), TURN LEFT AND PROCEED THROUGH TOWN, STAYING WITH US 60 & US 69 TOWARD **WHITE OAK** AND CHELSEA.

*Looking north on Wilson (then Main Street). The Hotel Vinita is on the left. Circa 1940s.*

*This old mill is still the most prominent landmark in White Oak.*

White Oak, whose school is proud home to the White Oak "Ranchers," and whose most prominent feature is the defunct White Oak Mill, is the next sign post on the highway. Founded near the turn of the century, a post office was opened here in 1898.

Named for the English home of railroad official Charles Peach, Chelsea was founded around 1870 and established a post office in November of 1882. The first oil well in Indian Territory was drilled

*Historic Route 66 bridge on Pryor Creek at Chelsea, built in 1926 by the Oklahoma State Highway Commission.*

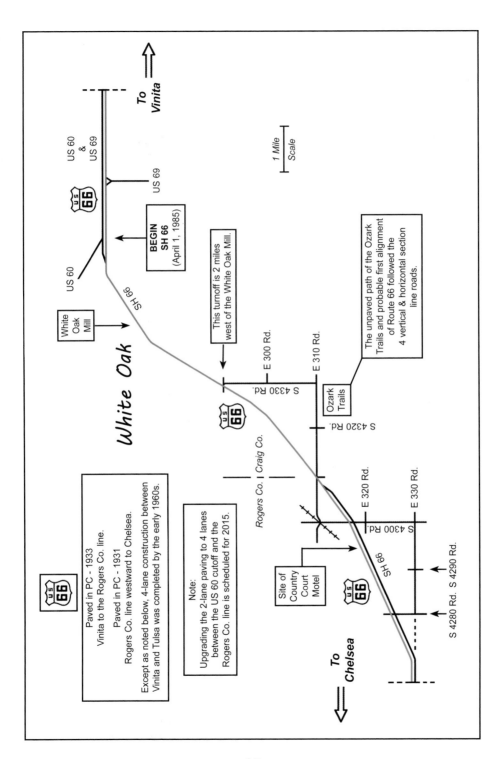

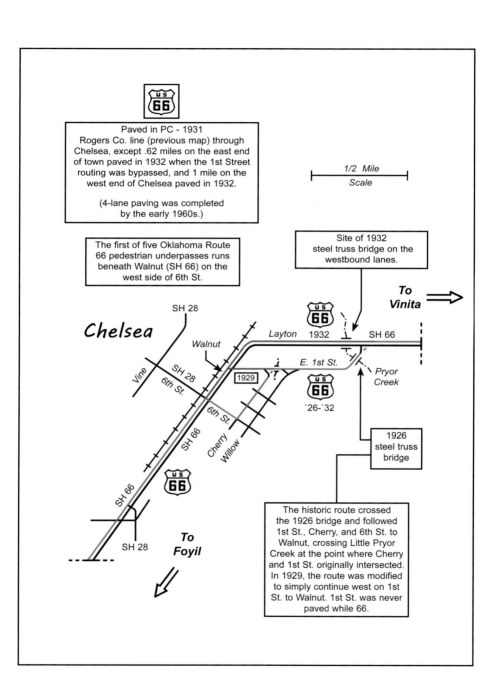

Paved in PC - 1931
Rogers Co. line (previous map) through
Chelsea, except .62 miles on the east end
of town paved in 1932 when the 1st Street
routing was bypassed, and 1 mile on the
west end of Chelsea paved in 1932.

(4-lane paving was completed
by the early 1960s.)

1/2 Mile
Scale

The first of five Oklahoma Route
66 pedestrian underpasses runs
beneath Walnut (SH 66) on the
west side of 6th St.

Site of 1932
steel truss bridge on the
westbound lanes.

To
Vinita

SH 28

Chelsea

Walnut

Layton

US 66

1932

SH 66

Vine

SH 28

6th St.

E. 1st St.

1929

US 66

`26-`32

Pryor
Creek

6th St.

SH 66

Cherry

Willow

1926
steel truss
bridge

SH 66

US 66

To
Foyil

SH 28

The historic route crossed
the 1926 bridge and followed
1st St., Cherry, and 6th St. to
Walnut, crossing Little Pryor
Creek at the point where Cherry
and 1st St. originally intersected.
In 1929, the route was modified
to simply continue west on 1st
St. to Walnut. 1st St. was never
paved while 66.

just west of town in 1889 by Edward Byrd, who had leased the land from the Cherokees. As a result, Chelsea and the surrounding area experienced immediate growth.

Will Rogers' sister, Sallie McSpadden, lived in Chelsea, as did Gene Autry for a time. Today, one of a diminishing number of historic "through" steel truss bridges on original Route 66 still straddles Pryor Creek at the east edge of the city. Located just south of SH 66, it has outlived its replacement on the main route. In town, at 10th

*Wall murals and similar attention-getters, like these at the Route 66 mall in Chelsea, are gaining in popularity all along the Mother Road.*

*Below: The Chelsea Motel accommodated its last guest many years ago.*

APPROACHING **CHELSEA**, TURN LEFT JUST BEFORE PRYOR CREEK TO ACCESS THE 1926 STEEL TRUSS BRIDGE AND FOLLOW THE EARLY ROUTE ON 1ST STREET TO WALNUT, THEN TURN LEFT AGAIN,
OR,
STAY ON THE PRESENT ALIGNMENT (SH 66) THROUGH CHELSEA TOWARD **BUSHYHEAD**.

*House ordered
from a
Sears & Roebuck
catalog at
10th & Olive
in Chelsea.*

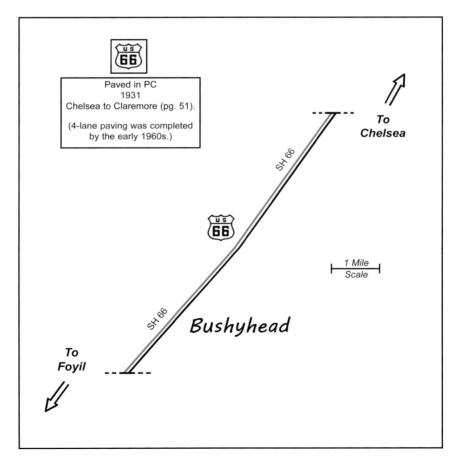

Paved in PC
1931
Chelsea to Claremore (pg. 51).

(4-lane paving was completed
by the early 1960s.)

SH 66

**To
Chelsea**

SH 66

*Bushyhead*

**To
Foyil**

1 Mile
Scale

Street and Olive, a house ordered by mail and assembled in 1913 from a Sears & Roebuck catalog still serves as a residence.

Keep an eye out for the tiny community of Bushyhead, which was named for Dennis W. Bushyhead, principal chief of the Cherokees from 1879-1887. This small hamlet had a post office from 1898 until 1955.

*Left:*
*Bushyhead—easy to miss.*

*Right:*
*Statue of Bunion Derby winner*
*Andrew Hartley Payne*
*in Foyil.*
Kathy Anderson

Nearby Foyil, founded in 1890, was named for its first postmaster, Alfred Foyil. Though one of the smaller cities on the Oklahoma route, Foyil is a mighty-mite when it comes to Mother Road distinctions. First, four miles east of town on SH 28A is Galloway Park, site of the world's tallest totem pole. Built by Ed Galloway in the early 1940s, the park, which contains a number of other totems, all made of concrete, was restored in the 1990s after decades of disrepair.

Foyil is also the hometown of Andy Payne, winner of one of the most remarkable events in sports history (see opposite). A statue honoring the town's favorite son can be found at the west end of the city on the highway's original alignment—Andy Payne Blvd.

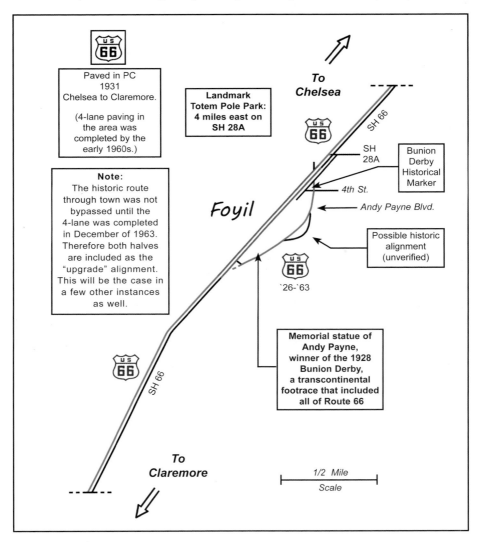

AT **FOYIL**, TURN LEFT JUST EAST OF TOWN AT THE JUNCTION WITH SH 28A, THEN IMMEDIATELY JOG RIGHT ONTO POPLAR, PARALLELING THE CURRENT HIGHWAY. AT THE "Y" IN FRONT OF THE HISTORICAL MARKER, BEAR LEFT ONTO ANDY PAYNE BLVD., OR,
STAY WITH SH 66 AND CONTINUE TOWARD **SEQUOYAH** AND CLAREMORE.

### THE BUNION DERBY

It was promoted as "C.C. Pyle's 1st Annual International Trans-Continental Footrace," and while it failed to become an annual event, the monumental marathon run in 1928 from Los Angeles to New York City not only made sports history, it proved

**"ANDY" PAYNE**

EDITION OF THE

**OFFICIAL PROGRAM**

*Andrew Payne crosses the Oklahoma state line ahead*

**C. C. PYLE'S**

PRICE 10 CENTS

First Annual
International
Trans-Continental
Footrace

*Andy at the Oklahoma state line.*
*All Bunion Derby images courtesy the late Vivian Payne*

to be the single most significant event Route 66 has known in terms of publicity.

Much of the highway then was either unpaved or under construction. Even so, making Route 66 America's premiere highway was the top priority for the US Highway 66 Association, and they pledged a large sum to support the promotion of a cross-country race that incorporated all of the route.

The man who accepted the challenge of staging the race, C.C. "Cash & Carry" Pyle, was both a sports entrepreneur of some renown and a self-styled showman. He saw it as a great opportunity to further his reputation and become wealthy in the process.

*Missouri billboard advertising the race.*

Headlined by a First Place prize of $25,000, "The Bunion Derby," as it came to be called, drew runners from around the world, among them internationally known champions and marathon record holders. There were over 200 entrants in all, ranging in age from 16 to 64. They came from as far away as Switzerland, the Philippines, and South Africa to take part. For the privilege of attempting the 3,400-mile long course, each entrant handed over $100 cash, a considerable sum at the time.

One of the hopefuls was Andy Payne, a 19-year-old part Cherokee farm boy from the Mother Road town of Foyil,

*Studio portrait of Andy Payne.*

Oklahoma. Andy was hardly considered a world-class runner, in fact, he had never participated in a race of greater stature than a state level track meet. He was, however, considered fleet-footed, at least by locals, and his friend John Woodward was once quoted as saying, "Andy was the best possum hunter and frog sticker I ever saw."

  With those attributes, Andy entered the great Bunion Derby, having trained on the back roads and in the fields near the family farm. Andy's reasons had little to do with fame or even a love for athletics. Rather they had more to do with helping his family and with his quest to become a man of means, whereby he could fulfill his dream of marrying his sweetheart and former teacher, Vivian.

  The race began with a boom at the Los Angeles Ascot Speedway on March 4, 1928. Runners were

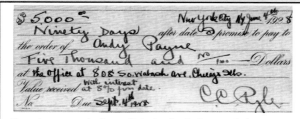

*C. C. Pyle,*
*Maestro of the Bunion Derby.*

required to cover a predetermined distance each day and were timed on how long they took getting there. Upon arrival at New York's Madison Square Garden, the participant with the shortest overall elapsed time would be the winner. Only the top ten finishers were eligible for prizes.

*Promissory note from Pyle to Andy for partial payment.*

  Early on, the focus of the press was almost exclusively on the more accomplished athletes, but as days became weeks the attention slowly shifted toward the unheralded young Oklahoman, who was consistently near the front of the pack, even as more seasoned contestants fell by the wayside.

  As the race reached his home state, Andy Payne had moved into the lead and was front page news coast to coast. His first-place position, though, was tenuous at best, as several other persistent challengers occasionally bested him on a given day's run. One of them—Peter "Iron Man" Gavuzzi—an Italian from Britain, finally overtook and then steadily pulled away from Andy as the tenacious marathoners chugged across Missouri.

Yet in the end, it was Andy Payne's perseverance, faith in himself, and good health that prevailed. Somewhere beyond the Ohio line, with Route 66 now behind them, the irrepressible Iron Man developed an abscessed tooth and faltered. Two days later he was forced to quit. By the time the remaining runners reached the Pennsylvania border, Andy's lead over second-place holder John Salo of New Jersey was an insurmountable 20 hours.

Hailed as the greatest victory in racing history, Andy, now 20, returned to Oklahoma a hero. With the prize money he paid off the family farm, bought land of his own, and married the lovely Vivian. After working in the newspaper business for a time, he went on to become Clerk of the Supreme Court of Oklahoma, a position he held for 38 years, until his retirement.

C.C. Pyle not only failed to get rich, he barely made expenses, and an attempt at a second race in 1929 drew little interest. Pyle died of a heart attack ten years later at age 57.

Aside from Andy Payne and the rest of the top ten finishers, the big winner of the Bunion Derby was the National US Highway 66 Association, as the on-going national publicity generated by the race succeeded in placing Route 66 squarely in the forefront in terms of highway recognition.

### THE BUNION DERBY — BY THE NUMBERS

Began—Sunday, March 4, 1928 - Los Angeles
Ended—Saturday, May 26, 1928 - New York City
Total Days—84
Total Distance—3423.3 miles
Support Entourage—More than 20 vehicles, including a custom-made Fageol touring bus used by C.C. Pyle.
Shortest Lap—16 miles (Ascot Speedway to Puente, CA.)
Longest Lap—74 miles (Bath, PA. to Deposit, NY.)
Number of Finishers—55
Entrants—between 199 and 256. Exact number unknown.
Winning Time—573 hours, 4 minutes, 34 seconds.

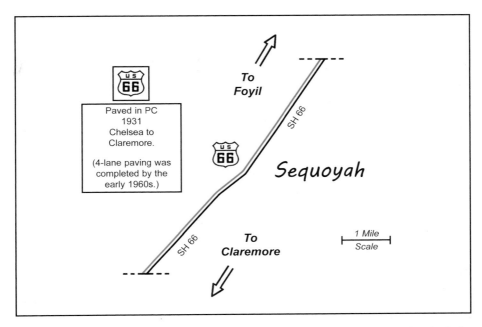

Named for the inventor of the Cherokee alphabet, the lightly inhabited farming community of Sequoyah dates all the way back to 1871, and while there may not be much here in the way of tourist attractions, Sequoyah closes the chapter on a pleasant and relaxing drive that began at Vinita. For only a few miles westward lies

*Sequoyah—waiting for the next train.*

Claremore, where there is enough to see and do to consume an entire day.

The home of Will Rogers, Claremore was founded in the early 1800s and named for Chief Clermont of the Osage tribe. The

*The Round-Up Motel in Claremore and its smoking cowboy are now gone.*

town's early years were marked by a historic battle between Osage settlers and a party of Cherokees, which took place northwest of the city on Claremore Mound in 1817.

Not long after the turn of the century, wildcatters drilling for oil tapped into an underground pool of sulphur water, and soon thereafter a number of enterprising towns- folk set about to capitalize on its

potential as a health aid by entering into the bath house business and offering a good soak for a modest sum.

Touted as "radium" water, and promising to cure (or at least improve) whatever maladies one might suffer, bath houses soon proliferated throughout town. And in spite of the water's pungent odor and unproven medical benefits, the baths maintained a presence in establish- ments as respected as the Will Rogers Hotel all the way into the 1970s.

Claremore may be best known as the home of our nation's favorite son, but the list of famous residents here does not end with Will Rogers. Among the city's other notable daughters and sons are playwright Lynn

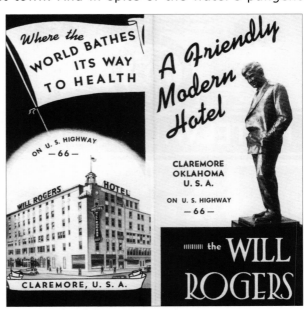

*Brochure from the heyday of Route 66 (and radium baths!)*
*Author's collection*

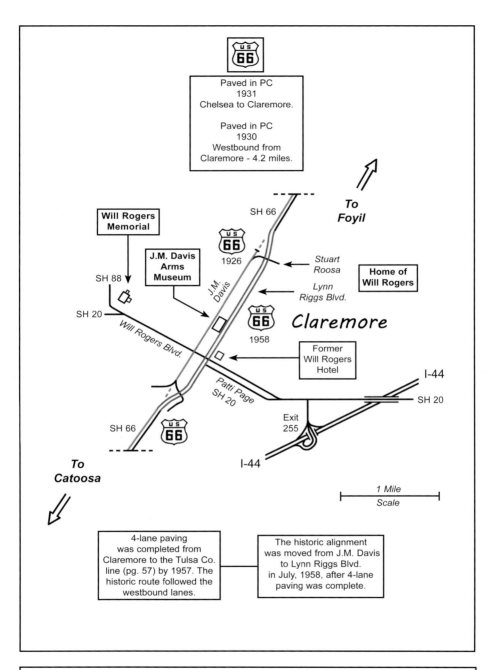

**US 66**

Paved in PC
1931
Chelsea to Claremore.

Paved in PC
1930
Westbound from
Claremore - 4.2 miles.

*To Foyil*

SH 66

**US 66** 1926

Will Rogers
Memorial

J.M. Davis
Arms
Museum

*Stuart
Roosa*

*Lynn
Riggs Blvd.*

Home of
Will Rogers

SH 88

SH 20

J.M. Davis

*Will Rogers Blvd.*

**US 66** 1958

*Claremore*

Former
Will Rogers
Hotel

I-44

SH 20

*Patti Page*
SH 20

Exit
255

SH 66

**US 66**

*To
Catoosa*

I-44

1 Mile
Scale

4-lane paving
was completed from
Claremore to the Tulsa Co.
line (pg. 57) by 1957. The
historic route followed the
westbound lanes.

The historic alignment
was moved from J.M. Davis
to Lynn Riggs Blvd.
in July, 1958, after 4-lane
paving was complete.

ENTERING **CLAREMORE**, TURN RIGHT AT THE INTERSECTION WITH STUART ROOSA TO FOLLOW J.M. DAVIS BLVD. THROUGH TOWN ON THE HISTORIC ROUTE,
OR,
STAY WITH SH 66 ON LYNN RIGGS BLVD. AND PROCEED TO **VERDIGRIS** AND CATOOSA.

Riggs (*Green Grow the Lilacs*, upon which the musical *Oklahoma* was based), astronaut Stuart Roosa, and country singing legend Patti Page.

Claremore is also home to a pair of world-class attractions. The first, of course, is the Will Rogers Memorial, located just a short distance from the historic route on Will Rogers Blvd. The second is the renowned J.M. Davis Arms and Historical Museum, which is said to house the world's largest collection of guns and associated artifacts, estimated at 20,000 pieces.

Even though old 66 through town is heavily commercialized these days, there are still a few reminders of the glory years, such as the Will Rogers Hotel and a couple of aging independent

*Above:*
*Radium bath houses once proliferated in Claremore. Ruins like this can still be found around town.*

motels on the west side of town.

The distance between Claremore and Catoosa is a little over ten miles and, except for the assortment of businesses strung along parts of it, is mostly flat and barren. En route, however, is another Route 66 community located just beyond the junction with SH 266. Verdigris, named for the nearby Verdigris River

*The original owner of this card wrote that they ate dinner here after touring the Will Rogers Memorial.*

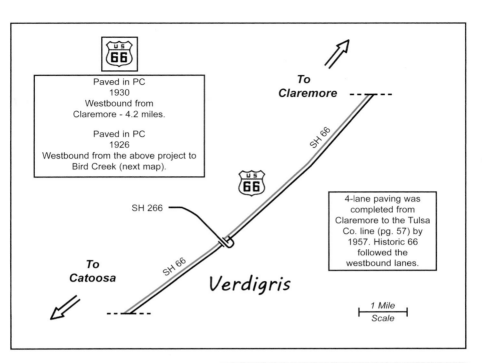

US 66

Paved in PC
1930
Westbound from
Claremore - 4.2 miles.

Paved in PC
1926
Westbound from the above project to
Bird Creek (next map).

To
Claremore

SH 66

US 66

SH 266

4-lane paving was
completed from
Claremore to the Tulsa
Co. line (pg. 57) by
1957. Historic 66
followed the
westbound lanes.

To
Catoosa

SH 66

Verdigris

1 Mile
Scale

*Right:*
*Railroad bridge over*
*the re-channeled*
*Verdigris River,*
*also known as the*
*McClellan-Kerr River*
*Navigation System.*

(the original channel of which has been re-named Bird Creek), first established a post office in 1880 and has become a growth area as a result of its proximity with the Tulsa metro. Just to the west, and virtually within view, are three substantial bridges (two for cars and one for locomotives) spanning the now divided waterway of the Verdigris.

First encountered is the massive railroad bridge, which stands alongside the almost unnoticeable modern spans that cross the

*A Transportation Department "Witness Post" marks the spot of a historic survey marker (lower left corner of photo and close-up below) along the right-of-way near the railroad bridge east of Catoosa.*

*The "almost twin" bridges over Bird Creek (formerly the Virdigris River) east of Catoosa. Railroad bridge is visible in the distance. Bridge on the left was replaced in 2011.*

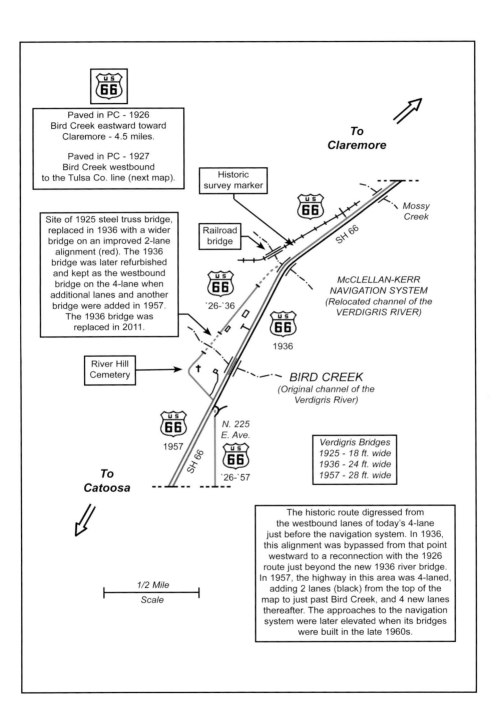

US 66

Paved in PC - 1926
Bird Creek eastward toward
Claremore - 4.5 miles.

Paved in PC - 1927
Bird Creek westbound
to the Tulsa Co. line (next map).

Site of 1925 steel truss bridge,
replaced in 1936 with a wider
bridge on an improved 2-lane
alignment (red). The 1936
bridge was later refurbished
and kept as the westbound
bridge on the 4-lane when
additional lanes and another
bridge were added in 1957.
The 1936 bridge was
replaced in 2011.

River Hill
Cemetery

To
Catoosa

1/2 Mile
Scale

Historic
survey marker

Railroad
bridge

US 66

US 66

'26-'36

US 66

1936

To
Claremore

Mossy
Creek

SH 66

McCLELLAN-KERR
NAVIGATION SYSTEM
(Relocated channel of the
VERDIGRIS RIVER)

BIRD CREEK
(Original channel of the
Verdigris River)

US 66

1957

SH 66

N. 225
E. Ave.

US 66

'26-'57

Verdigris Bridges
1925 - 18 ft. wide
1936 - 24 ft. wide
1957 - 28 ft. wide

The historic route digressed from
the westbound lanes of today's 4-lane
just before the navigation system. In 1936,
this alignment was bypassed from that point
westward to a reconnection with the 1926
route just beyond the new 1936 river bridge.
In 1957, the highway in this area was 4-laned,
adding 2 lanes (black) from the top of the
map to just past Bird Creek, and 4 new lanes
thereafter. The approaches to the navigation
system were later elevated when its bridges
were built in the late 1960s.

rechanneled river, which is part of the McClellan-Kerr Navigation System. Just ahead, as the road bends left, are the long-standing bridges over the original Verdigris River channel, now Bird Creek.

At a glance, the Bird Creek bridges appear identical, yet a closer look reveals that the westbound span is four feet skinnier than its eastbound counterpart. That is because it was actually built in 1936, then refurbished in 1957 when the eastbound lanes and

*River Hill Cemetery on the historic alignment near Catoosa.*

*Historic route near its first Verdigris River crossing at Catoosa.*

ENTERING **CATOOSA**, TURN RIGHT JUST PAST SPUNKY CREEK ONTO FORD, THEN TURN LEFT ONTO CHEROKEE, TAKING IT THOUGH TOWN ALL THE WAY TO THE INTERSECTION AT 193RD STREET AND TURN LEFT TO ADMIRAL PLACE,
OR,
STAY WITH SH 66 TO THE POINT WHERE IT MERGES WITH I-44 AND IMMEDIATELY BEAR RIGHT ONTO THE 193RD STREET EXIT. FROM THE OFF-RAMP, TURN LEFT ON 193RD.

an additional bridge were added. At that time, both were dedicated to former highway commissioner H. Tom Kight, Jr. Approvals for a project to replace the 1936 bridge got underway in 2010.

Just beyond Bird Creek, today's 4-lane is intersected by the original alignment (see previous map). A right turn at this point leads to a housing development on a stretch of first-generation PC that dead-ends near the original river crossing. A left turn from the 4-lane leads to a "Y" (swing right), then to a reconnection with the current route just past the former Arrowood's Trading Post (see map at right).

Some say the Cherokee word "Catoos" means "new settlement place." Others say it is a derivative of the Cherokee expression "Gi-tu-zi," which means, "here live the people of the light." In any event, it was from Catoos Hill that Catoosa acquired its name

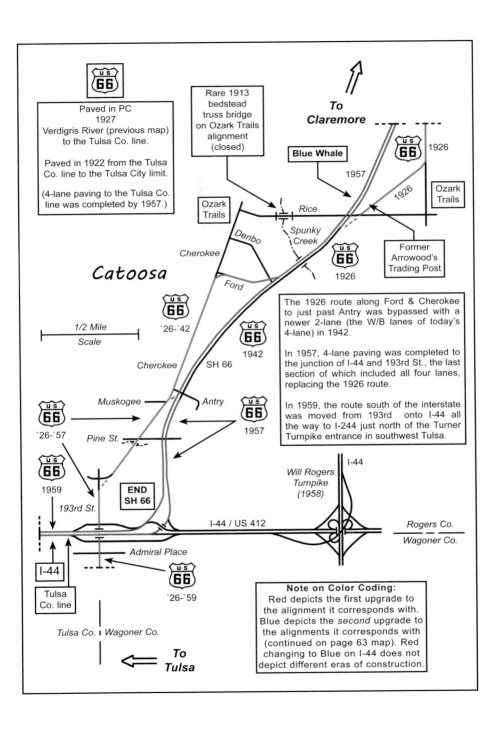

**US 66**

Paved in PC
1927
Verdigris River (previous map)
to the Tulsa Co. line.

Paved in 1922 from the Tulsa
Co. line to the Tulsa City limit.

(4-lane paving to the Tulsa Co.
line was completed by 1957.)

Rare 1913
bedstead
truss bridge
on Ozark Trails
alignment
(closed)

*To*
**Claremore**

Blue Whale

1957

**US 66** 1926

1926

Ozark
Trails

Ozark
Trails

Rice

Denbo

Spunky
Creek

Cherokee

**US 66**
1926

*Catoosa*

Ford

Former
Arrowood's
Trading Post

1/2 Mile
Scale

**US 66**
'26-'42

**US 66**
1942

The 1926 route along Ford & Cherokee
to just past Antry was bypassed with a
newer 2-lane (the W/B lanes of today's
4-lane) in 1942.

In 1957, 4-lane paving was completed to
the junction of I-44 and 193rd St., the last
section of which included all four lanes,
replacing the 1926 route.

Cherokee      SH 66

Muskogee         Antry

**US 66**
'26-'57

Pine St.

**US 66**
1957

In 1959, the route south of the interstate
was moved from 193rd onto I-44 all
the way to I-244 just north of the Turner
Turnpike entrance in southwest Tulsa.

**US 66**
1959

193rd St.

END
SH 66

I-44

*Will Rogers
Turnpike
(1958)*

I-44 / US 412

Rogers Co.

Wagoner Co.

I-44

Admiral Place

**US 66**
'26-'59

Tulsa
Co. line

Tulsa Co. ı Wagoner Co.

*To*
**Tulsa**

**Note on Color Coding:**
Red depicts the first upgrade to
the alignment it corresponds with.
Blue depicts the *second* upgrade to
the alignments it corresponds with
(continued on page 63 map). Red
changing to Blue on I-44 does not
depict different eras of construction.

*The former Arrowood Trading Post at Catoosa.*

during the expansion of the St. Louis-San Francisco Railroad in 1882.

Today, Catoosa is a legitimate seaport, serving as the inland terminus of the McClellan-Kerr Navigation System, which extends all the way to the Gulf of Mexico after linking with the Mississippi River. As the maps on pages 55 & 57 suggest, there is much to explore in the Catoosa area, including the original river crossing already described. Foremost, however, is the unmistakable Blue Whale, which is on the north side of the road atop the hill

*Left: Catoosa's Blue Whale in its heyday.*

*Facing Page: The Blue Whale before recent restoration.*

after coming off the Bird Creek bridges.

Built by Hugh Davis for his wife Zelta and their family on private property and completed around 1970, the big toothy whale and the pond it calls home provided outdoor fun for area children as well as adults for nearly twenty years, serving as both a gymnasium and diving platform. The park also included pint-sized picnic tables, a couple of boats, public rest rooms, a concession, and a landlocked ark of notable dimensions.

Following a decade of deterioration after its closing in the late 1980s, the grounds were cleaned up and the fading whale was refreshed with a coat of new paint. Most recently, the property has been looked after by Hugh Davis' son Blaine, who has taken up residence on-site. While the oversized playground is not officially open, visitors are permitted to browse around and take photos.

Hugh Davis was also brother-in-law to Chief Wolf Robe Hunt, a well-known jewelry craftsman and owner of a trading post on Route 66 in Tulsa. The two joined forces in establishing and operating a second trading post next to the Davis property in Catoosa. Years later, the Catoosa Indian Trading Post became Arrowood's, while the original trading post on Tulsa's 11th Street (Wolf-Robe's Indian Trading Post) became an antique shop called the Browsery (now gone). The Blue Whale, meanwhile, continues as a focal point, having become one of the most recognized landmarks and more popular stops on the tour.

Just beyond the Blue Whale, the next crossroad is the point where the original 1926 alignment angles in (see map on page 57).

This east-west road (Rice), is the Ozark Trails alignment, and if followed due west leads to a rare, one-lane 1913 bedstead truss bridge on Spunky Creek (now closed). It is possible that this road carried Route 66 traffic for a few months either as a temporary or detour route until first-generation paving begun in 1926 was completed in 1927. (It is not known whether the official route, which followed the path of the current highway to Ford Street, was in use prior to, or during, the paving process.) West of the 1913 bridge, Rice continues to a junction with Cherokee.

At the time, Catoosa's business center was on Cherokee to the east of Ford. City leaders tried in vain to persuade the Highway Commission to route US 66 traffic on Rice (then Alberty)

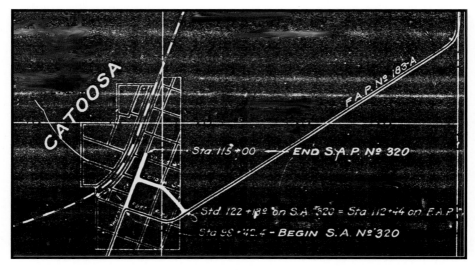

*This 1926 document shows the first official route into Catoosa, which followed the long diagonal line to connect with Ford (at the curve), then turned left onto Cherokee, which essentially bypassed the business district. The white, T-shaped lines represent the "spur" paving added by the state on Cherokee (top of "T"), and Denbo, (bottom of "T"). Note that mainline 66 has a Federal Aid Project number (FAP), while the spur is identified with a State Aid Project number (SAP).*
Oklahoma Department of Transportation

to Cherokee. As a compromise, the road was paved as planned, on Ford, with a macadam "spur" added at state expense that extended from Ford into the business district on Cherokee and also along Denbo back to its junction with US 66 where it connects with Ford.

In 1942, the Ford turnoff was bypassed when the road was extended from that point to connect with Cherokee just beyond Antry

*1913 bedstead truss bridge on Spunky Creek at Catoosa.*

(this change followed the path of today's westbound 4-lane). In 1957, Cherokee was bypassed altogether with the completion of 4-lane paving, which was needed to receive traffic expelled from the Will Rogers Turnpike (see map on page 57).

Today, whether following the route on Ford and Cherokee or the present 4-lane alignment on SH 66, the connection to the historic pathway into Tulsa at 193rd Street from Catoosa is a simple one to make.

Tulsa, the seat of Tulsa county and named for Alabama's Tulsey Town, opened its post office on March 25, 1879, and grew to become the state's second largest city. It is here that Route 66 was conceived, designed, and given life by Oklahoma State Highway Commissioner Cyrus Stevens Avery.

*North view at 193rd & Admiral in Tulsa, 1954, just south of today's I-44 overpass.*

*Oklahoma Department of Transportation*

61

*Right:*
*Originally Wolf-Robe's Indian Trading Post, Tulsa's Browsery was demolished in 1998.*

*Below:*
*The 66 Diner on Tulsa's 11th Street once served up good grub.*

Situated along the banks of the Arkansas River and once known as the oil capitol of the world, Tulsa's eastward expansion in the 1930s was due in large part to the Mother Road's 11th Street alignment. This long, straight stretch of highway ultimately became clogged with diners, motels, filling stations, and all manner of other

*Tulsa's Golden Drumstick was once a popular stop at 11th & Yale.*

FROM THE INTERSECTION OF 193RD AND ADMIRAL PLACE, STAY ON 193RD STREET SOUTH FOR ONE MILE TO EAST 11TH STREET AND TURN RIGHT TO ENTER **TULSA**. AT MINGO ROAD, THE HISTORIC ROUTE TURNS NORTH TO ADMIRAL PLACE AND CAN BE FOLLOWED USING THE MAPS, IF DESIRED.

TO FOLLOW THE MORE RECOMMENDED ROUTE, STAY WITH 11TH STREET ALL THE WAY TO DOWNTOWN TULSA (NEXT MAP).

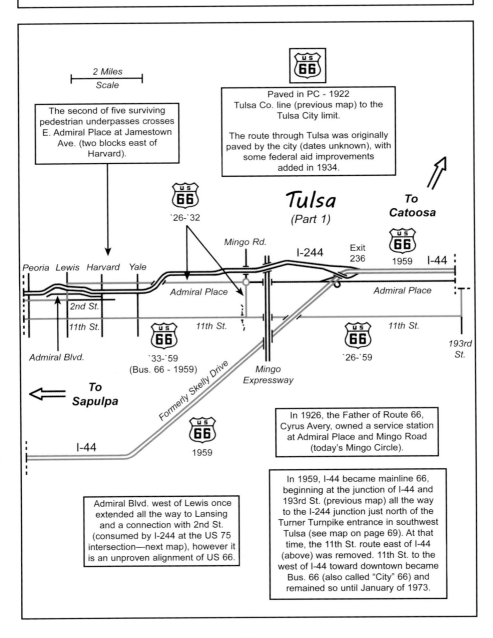

2 Miles
Scale

The second of five surviving pedestrian underpasses crosses E. Admiral Place at Jamestown Ave. (two blocks east of Harvard).

Paved in PC - 1922
Tulsa Co. line (previous map) to the Tulsa City limit.

The route through Tulsa was originally paved by the city (dates unknown), with some federal aid improvements added in 1934.

*Tulsa*
*(Part 1)*

To
Catoosa

Mingo Rd.

I-244

Exit 236

1959    I-44

'26-'32

Peoria  Lewis  Harvard  Yale

Admiral Place

Admiral Place

2nd St.

11th St.

11th St.

11th St.

193rd St.

Admiral Blvd.

'33-'59
(Bus. 66 - 1959)

'26-'59

Formerly Skelly Drive

Mingo Expressway

To
Sapulpa

In 1926, the Father of Route 66, Cyrus Avery, owned a service station at Admiral Place and Mingo Road (today's Mingo Circle).

I-44

1959

Admiral Blvd. west of Lewis once extended all the way to Lansing and a connection with 2nd St. (consumed by I-244 at the US 75 intersection—next map), however it is an unproven alignment of US 66.

In 1959, I-44 became mainline 66, beginning at the junction of I-44 and 193rd St. (previous map) all the way to the I-244 junction just north of the Turner Turnpike entrance in southwest Tulsa (see map on page 69). At that time, the 11th St. route east of I-44 (above) was removed. 11th St. to the west of I-44 toward downtown became Bus. 66 (also called "City" 66) and remained so until January of 1973.

AT THE INTERSECTION WITH ELGIN, ANGLE SLIGHTLY LEFT ONTO 10TH, WHICH CONVERTS BACK TO 11TH WEST OF BOULDER. JUST PAST DENVER, TURN LEFT ACROSS THE I-444 OVERPASS, THEN RIGHT ON 12TH. CONTINUE PAST THE STOP AT HOUSTON TO THE INTERSECTION AT SOUTHWEST BLVD. AND TURN LEFT TO CROSS THE ARKANSAS RIVER.

conveniences expected by motorists entering a town as stately as this one on their westward journey.

Today, both the Admiral Place and 11th Street routes remain heavily commercialized, and reminders from days gone by have become fewer in recent years. Even so, those with a watchful eye will spot plenty of relics, especially on 11th Street, all the way from 193rd in the east to near downtown.

Known for its wealth of Art Deco structures, Tulsa's central business district is still graced with many fine specimens, mingling

*Right:*
*Tulsa's 11th Street Bridge before being reconditioned as a historic landmark.*

*Below:*
*Engineer's rendering of the 1916 bridge, built in the Art Deco styling of the time.*

*Oklahoma Department of Transportation*

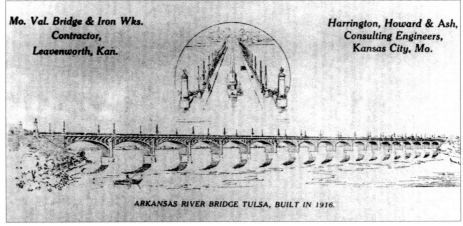

Mo. Val. Bridge & Iron Wks.
Contractor,
Leavenworth, Kan.

Harrington, Howard & Ash,
Consulting Engineers,
Kansas City, Mo.

ARKANSAS RIVER BRIDGE TULSA, BUILT IN 1916.

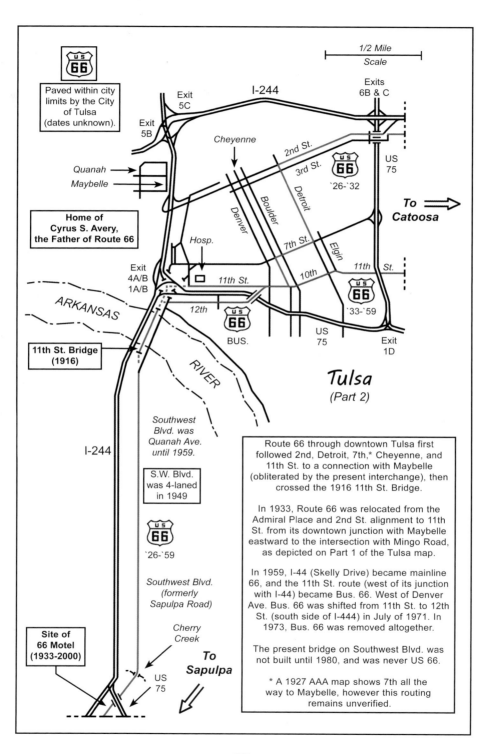

US 66

Paved within city
limits by the City
of Tulsa
(dates unknown).

1/2 Mile
Scale

Exit
5C

I-244

Exits
6B & C

Exit
5B

Cheyenne

2nd St.

3rd St.

US 66

US
75

Quanah

Maybelle

'26-'32

To
Catoosa

Home of
Cyrus S. Avery,
the Father of Route 66

Hosp.

Denver

Boulder

Detroit

7th St.

Elgin

11th   St.

Exit
4A/B
1A/B

11th St.

10th

US 66

ARKANSAS

12th

US 66

'33-'59

11th St. Bridge
(1916)

RIVER

US
75

BUS.

Exit
1D

Tulsa
*(Part 2)*

Southwest
Blvd. was
Quanah Ave.
until 1959.

I-244

S.W. Blvd.
was 4-laned
in 1949

US 66

'26-'59

Southwest Blvd.
*(formerly
Sapulpa Road)*

Site of
66 Motel
(1933-2000)

Cherry
Creek

To
**Sapulpa**

US
75

Route 66 through downtown Tulsa first
followed 2nd, Detroit, 7th,* Cheyenne, and
11th St. to a connection with Maybelle
(obliterated by the present interchange), then
crossed the 1916 11th St. Bridge.

In 1933, Route 66 was relocated from the
Admiral Place and 2nd St. alignment to 11th
St. from its downtown junction with Maybelle
eastward to the intersection with Mingo Road,
as depicted on Part 1 of the Tulsa map.

In 1959, I-44 (Skelly Drive) became mainline
66, and the 11th St. route (west of its junction
with I-44) became Bus. 66. West of Denver
Ave. Bus. 66 was shifted from 11th St. to 12th
St. (south side of I-444) in July of 1971. In
1973, Bus. 66 was removed altogether.

The present bridge on Southwest Blvd. was
not built until 1980, and was never US 66.

* A 1927 AAA map shows 7th all the
way to Maybelle, however this routing
remains unverified.

65

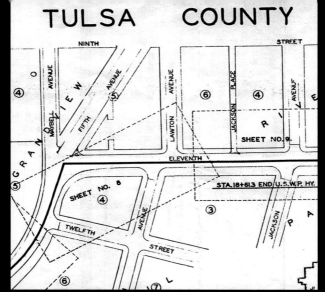

*Above: A 1936 detail map of downtown Tulsa shows US 66 connecting with Maybelle, where it turned south to cross the 1916 bridge. This pathway is represented as a dashed line on the map on page 65.*
*Below: A 1929 Tulsa inset map showing the historic routing of 66 following Admiral, Lewis, 2nd St., Detroit, 7th St., Cheyenne, and 11th St. to Maybelle.*
Oklahoma Department of Transportation

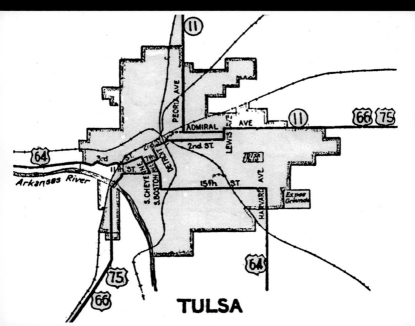

*Eastbound view on Southwest Blvd. from 25th Street, 1950. No trace of the buildings pictured remain today.*

Oklahoma Department of Transportation

comfortably with newer high-rises. Survivors to watch for near downtown on 11th St. are the Tulsa Monument Company and the Warehouse Market. Once across the river, Southwest Blvd. flows through a light commercial district where the old businesses have mostly been replaced with modern counterparts. Just beyond the underpass for US 75 is the site of the 66 Motel, a favorite Tulsa landmark until its destruction in 2001. It was replaced with a small warehouse.

*The 66 Motel was once one of Tulsa's most recognized and photographed Route 66 landmarks.*

*The Shady Rest Court once stood a couple of blocks west of the 66 Motel. It was razed in the mid-1990s after serving its final years as a flop house.*

AFTER CROSSING THE RIVER, CONTINUE ON SOUTHWEST BLVD. THROUGH **RED FORK**, **OAKHURST**, AND **BOWDEN** (NOW ON OLD SAPULPA RD.) TO THE T-INTERSECTION WITH SH 66 AT SAPULPA AND TURN RIGHT TO ENTER TOWN,
OR,
FOLLOW SOUTHWEST BLVD. TO S. 49TH W. AVE., TURN LEFT, PROCEED TO THE INTERCHANGE, ENTER I-44 WESTBOUND, AND IMMEDIATELY MOVE TO THE FAR LEFT LANE TO ACCESS SH 66 TO SAPULPA JUST BEFORE THE TURNPIKE ENTRANCE.

*This 1949 view is easterly just west of today's I-244 overpass on Southwest Blvd. (See top of map opposite). The row of buildings on the right still stands.*
Oklahoma Department of Transportation

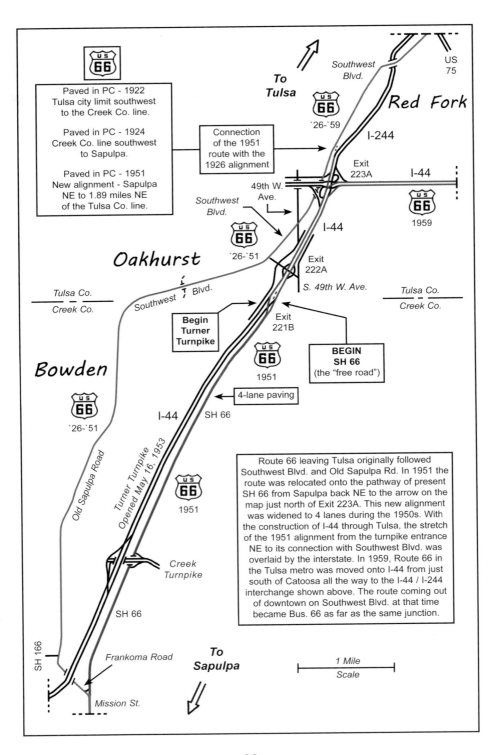

**US 66**

Paved in PC - 1922
Tulsa city limit southwest
to the Creek Co. line.

Paved in PC - 1924
Creek Co. line southwest
to Sapulpa.

Paved in PC - 1951
New alignment - Sapulpa
NE to 1.89 miles NE
of the Tulsa Co. line.

Connection
of the 1951
route with the
1926 alignment

To
Tulsa

Southwest
Blvd.

US
75

**US 66**
'26-'59

Red Fork

I-244

Exit
223A

I-44

49th W.
Ave.

**US 66**
1959

Southwest
Blvd.

I-44

**US 66**
'26-'51

Exit
222A

S. 49th W. Ave.

*Oakhurst*

Tulsa Co.
Creek Co.

Southwest    Blvd.

Tulsa Co.
Creek Co.

Begin
Turner
Turnpike

Exit
221B

**US 66**
1951

BEGIN
SH 66
(the "free road")

*Bowden*

**US 66**
'26-'51

4-lane paving

I-44    SH 66

Old Sapulpa Road

Turner Turnpike
Opened May 16, 1953

**US 66**
1951

Route 66 leaving Tulsa originally followed
Southwest Blvd. and Old Sapulpa Rd. In 1951 the
route was relocated onto the pathway of present
SH 66 from Sapulpa back NE to the arrow on the
map just north of Exit 223A. This new alignment
was widened to 4 lanes during the 1950s. With
the construction of I-44 through Tulsa, the stretch
of the 1951 alignment from the turnpike entrance
NE to its connection with Southwest Blvd. was
overlaid by the interstate. In 1959, Route 66 in
the Tulsa metro was moved onto I-44 from just
south of Catoosa all the way to the I-44 / I-244
interchange shown above. The route coming out
of downtown on Southwest Blvd. at that time
became Bus. 66 as far as the same junction.

Creek
Turnpike

SH 66

SH 166

Frankoma Road

To
Sapulpa

Mission St.

1 Mile
Scale

Red Fork, founded around 1884 and once known for its oil production during boomtown days, was named for the Red Fork of the Arkansas River. An industrial suburb during World War II, it was ultimately swallowed by the Tulsa metro.

The historic route leaving Tulsa toward Sapulpa is a pleasant drive alongside aging railroad tracks through countryside that has retained much of its old-time flavor. Here, it is easy to imagine encountering a string of bulky 1940s sedans, or pulling over for a bite at a greasy spoon, maybe in Oakhurst or Bowden. The road in places is worn and cracked and the few houses still clinging to the roadside are of the era. Leaving Tulsa as Southwest Blvd., this original path of US 66 changes unnoticeably to Old Sapulpa Road and finally to Frankoma Road nearing its connection with the newer 4-lane SH 66 at Sapulpa.

One of Sapulpa's heyday survivors,
its neon sign is now gone.

Sapulpa is the seat of Creek County and was named for James Sapulpa, a Creek Indian from Alabama who settled near Rock Creek in the mid-1800s and later opened a store. The Atlantic & Pacific Railroad arrived in 1886, and Sapulpa soon became a significant center for shipping cattle. Later, when oil was discovered, Sapulpa found itself part of the rich Glenn Pool field. Sapulpa in Creek means "sweet potato."

The first in a long string of towns bypassed by the 1953 opening of the Turner Turnpike,

ENTERING **SAPULPA**, SH 66 IS MISSION STREET. AT DEWEY AVENUE, TURN RIGHT AND CONTINUE THROUGH TOWN. AT THE WEST EDGE OF THE CITY, ACROSS FROM THE GOLF COURSE, THE HISTORIC ROUTE HOOKS OFF TO THE RIGHT AND CROSSES THE STEEL TRUSS BRIDGE ON ROCK CREEK. FOLLOW THIS ORIGINAL ALIGNMENT FOR THREE MILES TO ITS RECONNECTION WITH SH 66,
OR,
STAY WITH THE UPGRADE ALIGNMENT ON SH 66 TO **KELLYVILLE**.

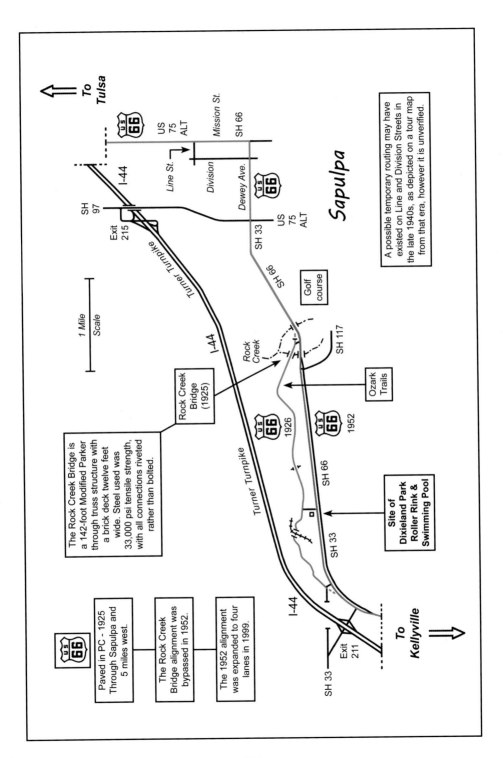

To Tulsa

US 66

I-44

SH 97

Exit 215

Turner Turnpike

US 75 ALT

Line St.

Mission St.

SH 66

Division

Dewey Ave.

US 75 ALT

SH 33

US 66

**Sapulpa**

A possible temporary routing may have existed on Line and Division Streets in the late 1940s, as depicted on a tour map from that era, however it is unverified.

1 Mile
Scale

Golf course

Rock Creek

SH 117

I-44

Rock Creek Bridge (1925)

The Rock Creek Bridge is a 142-foot Modified Parker through truss structure with a brick deck twelve feet wide. Steel used was 33,000 psi tensile strength, with all connections riveted rather than bolted.

Turner Turnpike

US 66
1926

US 66
1952

Ozark Trails

SH 66

SH 33

Site of Dixieland Park Roller Rink & Swimming Pool

I-44

US 66

Paved in PC - 1925 Through Sapulpa and 5 miles west.

The Rock Creek Bridge alignment was bypassed in 1952.

The 1952 alignment was expanded to four lanes in 1999.

SH 33

Exit 211

To Kellyville

Sapulpa not only survived, but today is one of the more vibrant cities on the route. Pride in Route 66 here remains solid, evidenced by reminders of the historic highway displayed throughout town.

A crown jewel of the Oklahoma road awaits at the west end of the city, where old 66 crosses the Rock Creek Bridge and drifts away from civilization to meander through wooded terrain in the shadow of the railroad. The weathered pavement here is a direct throwback to the days when the road stuck to the lay of the land, irrespective of its unruly configuration. This is especially evident

*Left:*
*Sapulpa's Happy Burger.*

*Below:*
*The 1925 Rock Creek Bridge at Sapulpa—an enduring landmark.*

near the far end of this loop, where a series of graceful but sharp S-curves speak to the danger that existed in the days of jalopies and low visibility.

Along the way, just before the railroad trestle, is the ruin of Dixieland Park, nestled on a side road between the highway's two alignments. Built in the 1920s and once a haven for the well-to-do, the park consisted of a pool, roller rink, cabins, cafe, and a station. The pool, once filled with the shrieks of children and the twang of springboards, ended up a mute boneyard for the rusting husks of old cars until it was eventually filled in. Only the poolhouse building survives.

From the rejoining of the two alignments, the drive to Kellyville is a short one. En route, a couple of miles east of town, a row of old rock cabins once sat stoically in a fenced pasture on the south side of the highway. Weed-infested and collapsing, their usefulness to tourists long past, they were finally razed in 2007 after the land was sold.

Kellyville, named for local merchant James E. Kelly, opened its post office in 1893. The old cotton gin remains a prominent feature

*This old cabin and its decrepit companions, originally built as Rock Lake Courts east of Kellyville, were destroyed after the property was sold in 2007.*

here, though it hasn't processed any cotton in years. At the east end of town, remnants of first-generation paving can be seen on the right just before the old road angles across to the south and onto Oak St., where it soon becomes impassable. West of town, near Little Polecat

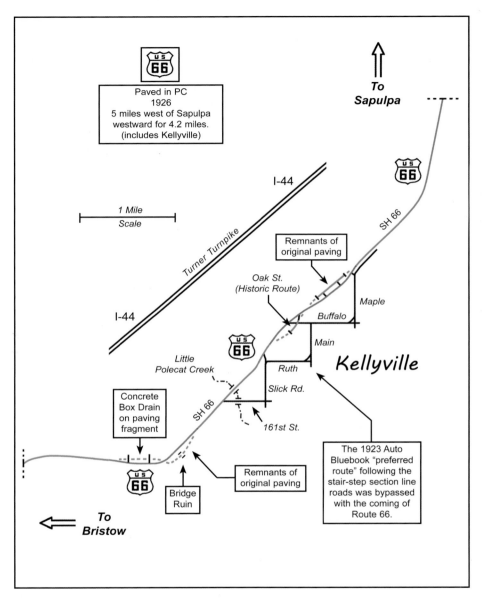

Paved in PC
1926
5 miles west of Sapulpa
westward for 4.2 miles.
(includes Kellyville)

To
Sapulpa

I-44

1 Mile
Scale

Turner Turnpike

Remnants of
original paving

SH 66

I-44

Oak St.
(Historic Route)

Maple

Buffalo

Main

Little
Polecat Creek

Ruth

Kellyville

Slick Rd.

Concrete
Box Drain
on paving
fragment

SH 66

161st St.

The 1923 Auto
Bluebook "preferred
route" following the
stair-step section line
roads was bypassed
with the coming of
Route 66.

Remnants of
original paving

Bridge
Ruin

To
Bristow

Creek, there is an old factory that was once a whistle stop for the railroad, and on both ends of the upcoming curve, a keen eye will once again catch glimpses of old Portland Concrete interlacing with the current road.

Just west of the I-44 overpass (next map) is the first of three closely connected sections of original concrete roadway bypassed in

*Abandoned station east of Kellyville, photographed in 1954.*
*US 66 traffic dwindled following the 1953 opening of the Turner Turnpike.*
Archives & Manuscripts Division, Oklahoma Historical Society

*Below:*
*Exaggerated signs like this one next*
*to Little Polecat Creek just west of*
*Kellyville were once common all along*
*Route 66.*

*A Federal Aid Project (FAP) marker,*
*brass shield intact, lies in a ditch near*
*Kellyville, having apparently worked*
*itself free from the earth.*

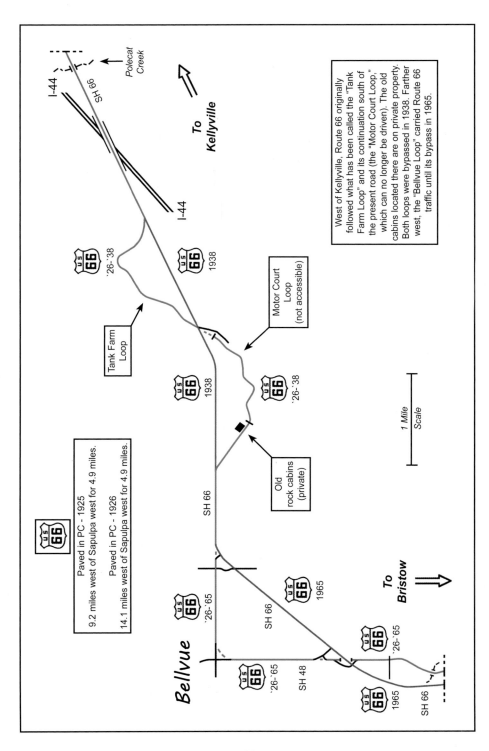

Bellvue

Paved in PC - 1925
9.2 miles west of Sapulpa west for 4.9 miles.

Paved in PC - 1926
14.1 miles west of Sapulpa west for 4.9 miles.

Tank Farm Loop

Motor Court Loop
(not accessible)

Old rock cabins
(private)

SH 66

I-44

SH 66

Polecat Creek

'26-'38

1938

1938

'26-'38

To Kellyville

'26-'65

SH 66

1965

SH 48

'26-'65

'26-'65

1965

SH 66

To Bristow

1 Mile
Scale

West of Kellyville, Route 66 originally followed what has been called the "Tank Farm Loop" and its continuation south of the present road (the "Motor Court Loop," which can no longer be driven). The old cabins located there are on private property. Both loops were bypassed in 1938. Farther west, the "Bellvue Loop" carried Route 66 traffic until its bypass in 1965.

favor of the present alignment. The first is known as the Tank Farm Loop, so named because of the number of oil leases along the right-of-way. Here, motorists have a chance to briefly escape the present and re-experience the days before highways had shoulders and negotiating each curve involved some level of risk.

At the point of reconnection, the original road continued on the opposite side of the present highway, but is now inaccessible.

CONTINUING WEST FROM KELLYVILLE ON SH 66, CROSS OVER THE TURNPIKE (I-44), THEN WATCH FOR THE OLD CONCRETE ALIGNMENT ANGLING OFF TO THE RIGHT. FOLLOW THIS HISTORIC LOOP FOR APPROXIMATELY 2 MILES TO A RECONNECTION WITH THE CURRENT ROUTE,
OR,
STAY WITH SH 66 WESTBOUND.

A FEW MILES FARTHER ALONG, AGAIN WATCH FOR OLD CONCRETE HOOKING OFF TO THE RIGHT. DRIVE THIS ALIGNMENT TO THE JUNCTION WITH SH 48 AT **BELLVUE**, TURN LEFT, THEN PROCEED TO A RECONNECTION WITH CURRENT SH 66 AND TURN RIGHT, OR, CONTINUE ON SH 66 INTO **BRISTOW**.

*Originally the Wildhorse Prairie Cabins, this motor court turned residence east of Bristow is on private property.*

Called the Motor Court Loop, for lack of a more descriptive name, it is approximately two miles in length and has the distinction of being the longest privately owned strip of intact Route 66 in Oklahoma. Near its west end, a row of finely crafted rock cabins stand like saluting soldiers. Closed to tourists for decades, today they serve as a home and storage space to the property owner.

Only a mile farther west, the old highway again slips off to the right, heading due west. This digression is appropriately called

IN BRISTOW, TURN RIGHT AT 4TH STREET AND CONTINUE ON SH 66 TOWARD DEPEW, OR, EXPLORE THE EARLY ROUTE (WITH CAUTION) USING THE MAP ON PAGE 79.

the Bellvue Loop in honor of the community located at the intersection where old 66 abruptly turns back south on what is now SH 48. Named for the Bellvue School (1909), which in turn had been named by county superintendent P.T. Fry, Bellvue opened its post office in 1913. On a hill at the crossroad here, there remains a building constructed of logs as an identifying landmark. From that point to its connection with SH 66, newer paving has overlaid the old.

The Tank Farm and Motor Court Loops were both bypassed in 1938, only twelve years after their paving, possibly due to terrain or newer standards for road width. The Bellvue Loop, however, continued to carry mainline traffic until its bypass in 1965.

From the place where the last leg of the Bellvue Loop (SH 48) intersects the present road (SH 66), it is possible to stay with the historic alignment by accessing its continuation on the south side of

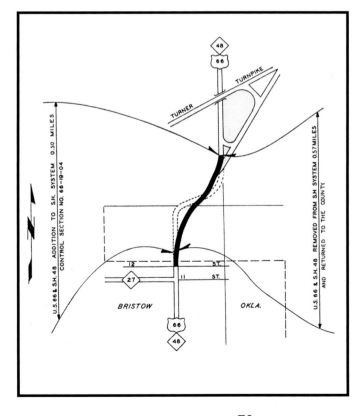

This 1960 document shows the original path of 66 entering Bristow before it was straightened (heavy black line). Its location is just west of the turnpike overpass in the area of the Sand Creek Bridge.

Oklahoma Department of Transportation

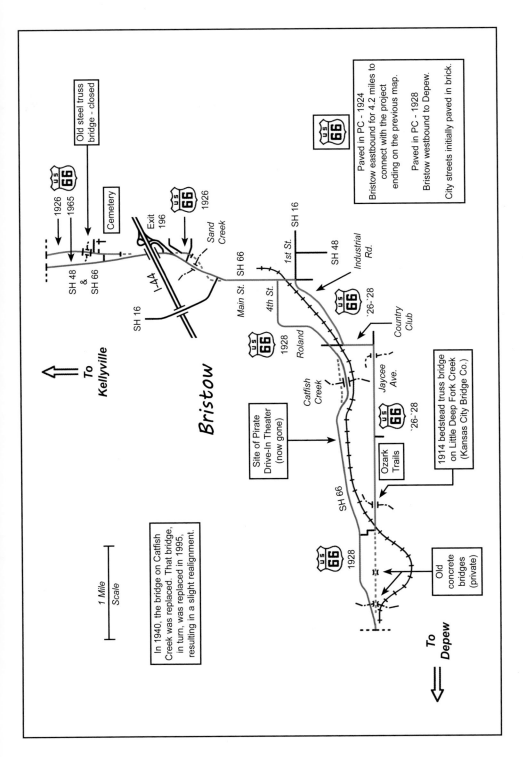

Old steel truss bridge - closed

1926
1965

Cemetery

1926

Sand Creek

Exit 196

SH 48 & SH 66

I-44

SH 16

Main St. SH 66

4th St.

Roland

1928

Catfish Creek

1st St.

SH 16

SH 48

Industrial Rd.

'26-'28

Country Club

Jaycee Ave.

'26-'28

Ozark Trails

SH 66

1928

Site of Pirate Drive-In Theater (now gone)

1914 bedstead truss bridge on Little Deep Fork Creek (Kansas City Bridge Co.)

Old concrete bridges (private)

To Kellyville

Bristow

To Depew

1 Mile Scale

In 1940, the bridge on Catfish Creek was replaced. That bridge, in turn, was replaced in 1995, resulting in a slight realignment.

Paved in PC - 1924 Bristow eastbound for 4.2 miles to connect with the project ending on the previous map.

Paved in PC - 1928 Bristow westbound to Depew.

City streets initially paved in brick.

*Built by the Kansas City Bridge Co., this rare 1914 "bedstead" steel truss span on Little Deep Fork Creek is still in use on the historic alignment just west of Bristow.*

*The Gold Eagle was a hot spot in 1940s Bristow.*
*Laurel Kane collection*

the newer road, as shown on the map on page 76. However this route will dead-end at a closed bridge near the cemetery (map on page 79), so a bit of backtracking will be necessary.

Bristow, which began as a trading post around 1897 in Indian Territory, became a town in 1901 and was named for Assistant Postmaster General J.L. Bristow. Like many other Oklahoma cities initially established along the rail lines, oil and gas soon figured prominently in the town's growth. Streets still paved in brick are a noteworthy feature of this bustling Route 66 city. Landmarks include

*This vintage station, presently the Bristow Firestone, has changed names and colors over the years, but seems to be as resiliant as the road itself.*

*Right:*
*One of two concrete bridge ruins on the unpaved historic route west of the steel truss bridge above—now on private property.*

the former Bristow Motor Company, originally a Ford dealership dating to 1923, and the recently restored train depot.

Leaving Bristow, the original alignment did not turn right at 4th Street. Instead it continued across the tracks to follow the path of the Ozark Trails, and can be driven until it becomes impassable just beyond the railroad crossing next to the 1914 bridge (see map on page 79). There, a connecting road leads back to present SH 66.

*Vintage station in downtown Depew.*

Approaching Depew, the historic route followed the section line dogleg from 1926-1928, as shown on the map opposite. This was eliminated when the route was paved.

Originally called Halls by the railroad, Depew established a post office in 1901 and was named for New York senator Chauncey M. Depew. Another hard-nosed survivor of the turnpike bypass, Depew's business district offers many fine examples of vintage architecture dating back to the early part of the century.

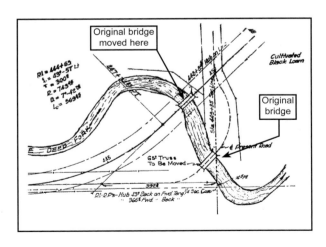

*This 1925 document shows the proposed realignment of then SH 7 on its approach to Depew. The existing road followed the north/south section line, then swung out to cross the creek. In 1928, the improved alignment (by then US 66) was completed. The existing bridge was moved, and remained on the present road until finally being replaced in 1973.*

*Oklahoma Department of Transportation*

AT **DEPEW**, TURN LEFT FROM SH 66 ONTO FLYNN TO HORSESHOE THROUGH TOWN ON MAIN AND LADD, THEN RESUME ON SH 66 WESTBOUND TOWARD STROUD.

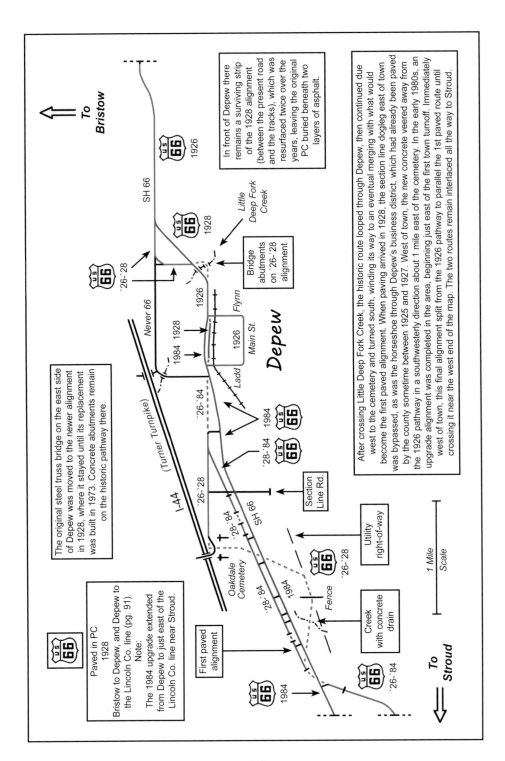

To **Bristow**

SH 66

1926

1928

'26-'28

Never 66

1984 1928

1926

1926

Flynn

Ladd

Main St.

*Depew*

Little
Deep Fork
Creek

Bridge abutments
on '26-'28
alignment

In front of Depew there remains a surviving strip of the 1928 alignment (between the present road and the tracks), which was resurfaced twice over the years, leaving the original PC buried beneath two layers of asphalt.

The original steel truss bridge on the east side of Depew was moved to the newer alignment in 1928, where it stayed until its replacement was built in 1973. Concrete abutments remain on the historic pathway there.

(Turner Turnpike)

I-44

'26-'28

'26-'84

'28-'84

SH 66

Section
Line Rd.

1984

'28-'84

1984

Utility
right-of-way

'26-'28

Oakdale
Cemetery

'28-'84

1984

Fence

Creek
with concrete
drain

First paved
alignment

1984

'26-'84

Paved in PC
1928
Bristow to Depew, and Depew to the Lincoln Co. line (pg. 91).
Note:
The 1984 upgrade extended from Depew to just east of the Lincoln Co. line near Stroud.

After crossing Little Deep Fork Creek, the historic route looped through Depew, then continued due west to the cemetery and turned south, winding its way to an eventual merging with what would become the first paved alignment. When paving arrived in 1928, the section line dogleg east of town was bypassed, as was the horseshoe through Depew's business district, which had already been paved by the county sometime between 1925 and 1927. West of town, the new concrete veered away from the 1926 pathway in a southwesterly direction about 1 mile east of the cemetery. In the early 1980s, an upgrade alignment was completed in the area, beginning just east of the first town turnoff. Immediately west of town, this final alignment split from the 1926 pathway to parallel the 1st paved route until crossing it near the west end of the map. The two routes remain interlaced all the way to Stroud.

1 Mile
Scale

To
**Stroud**

83

## — R E S T  S T O P —

### FORGOTTEN HIGHWAY

It was June of 1999, and I had planned a trip to Catoosa to chart a short stretch of Portland Concrete recently discovered by (then) Oklahoma Association Secretary Kathy Anderson. That same month, I had unexpectedly received from ODOT a couple of intriguing 1971 aerial photos taken near Depew that had been marked for disposal. Depew was a location I'd had long-standing questions about concerning the highway's first alignment, so I welcomed the photos, hopeful they might reveal a secret or two.

Under close examination, my attention was drawn to a faint line running through the woodland west of town. I reasoned that it could be a fence line or a utility right-of-way. But I also knew it could be the remaining traces of a road, and that was enough for me to schedule a stop there on my upcoming run to Catoosa. I invited Kathy to come along.

It was late in the day when we arrived there on the return trip. We began by tracing the 1926 route where it was accessible just west of Depew, hoping to determine whether this pathway (1) stuck with the first paved route where it angled away from its due west trek, (2) turned back south toward the upgrade alignment at the next intersecting road west of (1), or (3) that it possibly continued due west to an unknown point of reconnection. If option (2) or (3) turned out to be the case, we would then try to locate the exact point where the two alignments rejoined.

While comparing the aerial photo to the physical location, the first thing I discovered was that the north-south intersecting road was not where it belonged. The photo showed it to be farther west, near a cemetery. Obviously, if it didn't exist in 1971, it couldn't possibly have been part of the historic route. That ruled out option (2) above. At this point we knew we were on to something, we just didn't know what.

We proceeded to the cemetery, but once there found not even a hint of a roadway heading south, as depicted on the aerial. Following more discussion and some head scratching, we turned about, figuring to forage along the upgrade alignment for the possible missing link in the 1926 route.

Close scrutiny paid off. We found a swath through the trees exactly where a road from the cemetery would have met the paved alignment. But it didn't end there. Its path could be faintly seen continuing across a fenced pasture and into some trees on

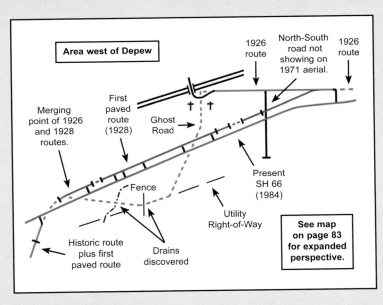

the south side of the highway. Option (1) couldn't yet be ruled out, but was looking weaker by the minute.

Next we drove west on present SH 66, then turned south onto the first paved route where it once crossed the current road. We reasoned that the ghost road would have reconnected in that area, which was beyond the boundary of the aerial photo. We found nothing, though, and finally called it a day.

Encouraged, I performed a computer search of US Geological Survey aerials and got lucky, finding a wider-ranging photo that not only revealed the rejoining of the two alignments, but also showed the existence of a ravine crossing the ghost road. This meant the possibility of a bridge.

Several days later I returned to the site, armed with a fistful of documentation, a camera, and a compass. My goal was to find evidence of a structure on that ravine. Despite the dark mist that kept my wipers working all the way there, my direction of travel made spotting the cut through the foliage fairly easy.

I parked and started out, happy to find no fence and a

*Concrete drain found under the historic alignment west of Depew.*

clear path to follow. I now had little doubt that this well-defined tunnel through the trees had carried traffic at one time, and that contention was soon strengthened as I began to find corroded tin cans embedded in the soil.

At the ravine, I was met with a sharp drop-off to a trickling creek twelve feet below, but found no trace of a bridge structure, timber or otherwise. Disappointed, but not willing to give up, I decided to keep going, so I made my way down the slope, crossed the creek by way of a fallen tree, and climbed the opposite bank.

I found more cans, then encountered a fence just east of the swath's junction with a utility right-of-way. Only a stone's throw across that fence stood an old wooden pole. I was just curious enough about it to hop over for a closer look, and that proved to make all the difference. For right next to that pole I found a small, weathered, concrete drain, all but proving the existence of a road. I felt like thumping my chest; instead I snapped a picture and then headed back toward the creek.

There, I meandered downward again, this time taking a slightly different path than before—a change that led to a second, and final, discovery. The bank here was steeper, and it took only a couple of steps before the wet leaves caused me to slip and take a short fall—short because I was stopped by a large rock draped in foliage. When I recovered from the blow and righted myself to a sitting position, I found myself looking directly down the throat of another concrete drain. I was so amazed that momentarily the pain in my shoulder was forgotten as I just sat there, staring.

The drain was offset several feet from the present creek channel and dry. I thought it over and finally decided that road builders of the time had installed the drain and then back-filled the chasm rather than build a bridge. Over the decades, the creek channel had shifted and slowly eroded the fill, leaving the gorge that existed next to the drain. That theory at first seemed a bit of a stretch, but considering that this alignment was never paved and had been without maintenance for 70 years, it was not unrealistic.

To put a wrap on it, I asked ODOT to try to verify my findings. Days later I had my answer. A construction plan for the 1928 first paved alignment had been located, and the drawings included the "existing" road, which matched up exactly to the ghost road I had hiked. While it was a gratifying and important find, I couldn't help but wonder how many other bones of that dinosaur known as original Route 66 were still hidden away, and how many of them I would be lucky enough to discover. Of one thing I was fairly certain: there would be more detective work waiting somewhere down the road.

*Old drain (concealed under rocks) discovered at creek on ghost road west of Depew.*

A close look at the map on page 83 makes it apparent that much exploring can be done along the rather complex mix of alignments that spring westward from Depew. This remains true all the way to Stroud, evidenced by the map below and the succeeding map on page 91. Many of these snippets of abandoned pavement can be driven, although most are discontinuous or cross private property and are inaccessible.

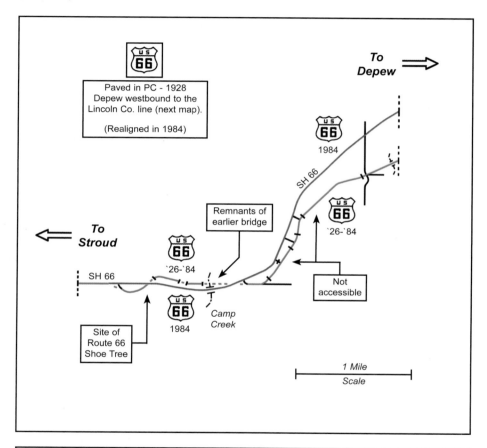

To Depew

Paved in PC - 1928
Depew westbound to the
Lincoln Co. line (next map).

(Realigned in 1984)

1984

SH 66

To
Stroud

Remnants of
earlier bridge

'26-'84

'26-'84

SH 66

Not
accessible

1984

Camp
Creek

Site of
Route 66
Shoe Tree

1 Mile
Scale

CONTINUING WESTBOUND FROM DEPEW TO STROUD, SIMPLY STAY WITH SH 66.

The terrain in this area is a blend of pasture and woodland, where original paving sticks to the contours of the land, dipping and climbing as it goes. Surprisingly, the first-generation concrete roadway here was not straightened until 1984, barely a year before its redesignation from US 66 to SH 66.

*This unusual stone arch bridge, now on private property, is depicted on the extreme right on the map opposite.*

All across Oklahoma, as elsewhere, Route 66 is known for its diversity, not only because of vastly changing scenery and its many pathways, but in the adventure of never knowing what may await just ahead. It has been said that one only needs to drive a few miles of America's Main Street and almost everything changes—the highway, the lay of the land, and the attractions and icons that together make the experience unique.

*Lonesome roadbed west of Depew.*

One current oddity of the Oklahoma road, the Route 66 Shoe Tree, can be found at the junction of the old and new alignments about a half-mile west of Camp Creek at the entrance to a historic loop of roadway on the left (see map opposite). Though this very short but delightful stretch of tarnished paving now resides on private property, it is presently open to vehicles, and motorists are invited to hang a pair of footwear in the tree, should the urge strike.

*This steel truss bridge by J.B. Klein Foundry of Oklahoma City spans Salt Creek on the first paved alignment just east of Stroud.*

STAY WITH SH 66 THROUGH **STROUD** TO DAVENPORT (PAGE 93), OR,
FOR THE EARLY ROUTE LEAVING STROUD, PART OF WHICH IS UNPAVED, TURN LEFT AT SH 99, THEN RIGHT ON CENTRAL UNTIL IT TURNS SOUTH AT THE RAILROAD TRACKS. TURN RIGHT AT THE NEXT CROSSROAD, PROCEED 1 MILE, THEN LEFT 1 MILE TO THE OZARK TRAILS OBELISK (SEE PAGE 93), THEN RIGHT HERE 2 MILES TO REJOIN SH 66 AFTER CROSSING THE REPLACEMENT BRIDGE ON DOSIE CREEK.

Stroud, founded in 1892 not far from Indian Territory by well-known trader James Stroud, quickly grew and prospered from the sale of illicit whiskey smuggled to Indians and sold to celebrating cowboys passing through. By the time statehood rolled around in 1907, the city boasted nine operating saloons. When Oklahoma joined the nation however, it came in dry, and the economic focus of the town was forced to shift. Ultimately, agriculture and oil became Stroud's two primary commodities.

*Downtown Stroud, circa 1940s.*

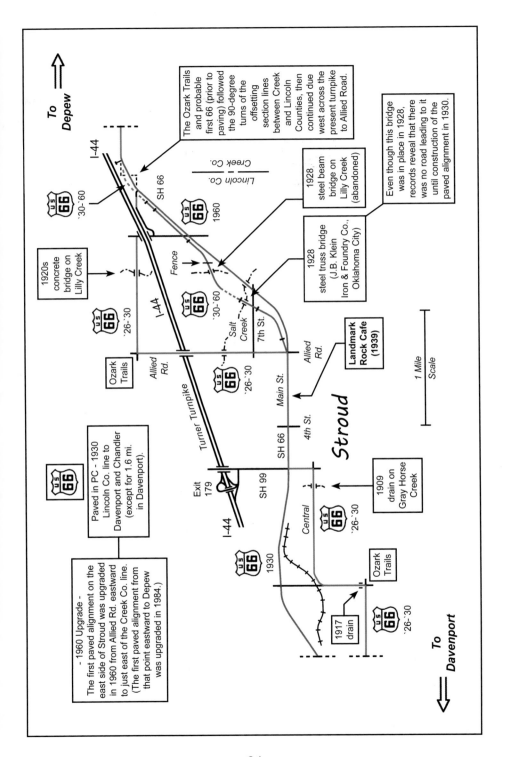

To **Depew**

I-44

The Ozark Trails and probable first 66 (prior to paving) followed the 90-degree turns of the offsetting section lines between Creek and Lincoln Counties, then continued due west across the present turnpike to Allied Road.

SH 66

*Lincoln Co.*
*Creek Co.*

1928 steel beam bridge on Lilly Creek (abandoned)

1920s concrete bridge on Lilly Creek

*Fence*

1928 steel truss bridge (J.B. Klein Iron & Foundry Co., Oklahoma City)

Even though this bridge was in place in 1928, records reveal that there was no road leading to it until construction of the paved alignment in 1930.

'30-'60

US 66

1960

US 66

'26-'30

I-44

US 66

'30-'60

*Salt Creek*

7th St.

Ozark Trails

*Allied Rd.*

**Turner Turnpike**

*Allied Rd.*

**Landmark Rock Cafe (1939)**

US 66

'26-'30

*Main St.*

**Stroud**

1 Mile

Scale

Paved in PC - 1930 Lincoln Co. line to Davenport and Chandler (except for 1.6 mi. in Davenport).

US 66

Exit 179

SH 99

SH 66

4th St.

*Central*

US 66

'26-'30

1909 drain on Gray Horse Creek

I-44

US 66

1930

- 1960 Upgrade -
The first paved alignment on the east side of Stroud was upgraded in 1960 from Allied Rd. eastward to just east of the Creek Co. line. (The first paved alignment from that point eastward to Depew was upgraded in 1984.)

Ozark Trails

US 66

'26-'30

1917 drain

To **Davenport**

91

*Stroud's Rock Cafe, a favorite stop since 1939.*

Today, Route 66 as Main Street stabs arrow-straight through the heart of the business district. There are a total of two traffic lights in town, and the boulevard itself is a textbook example of small town America. Here, a scattering of neon signs still pulse at sundown, and at the east end of Main St. the Rock Cafe, cornerstone of the town and since 1939 one of the Mother Road's more enduring landmarks, anchors Stroud firmly to the highway.

Continuing west, about halfway between Stroud and Davenport a significant landmark remains on the historic alignment—an Ozark Trails obelisk. One of only seven still in existence, it has been standing sentry on these famous motor routes since 1921.

Named by the town's first postmistress, Nettie Davenport, for her family, Davenport established a post office in 1892. Initially a farming community, the town saw growth when oil was discovered nearby in 1924, and has endured since.

*The 1917 steel truss bridge on Dosie Creek east of Davenport was demolished in 2004.*

STAY WITH SH 66 THROUGH **DAVENPORT** AND CONTINUE TOWARD CHANDLER.

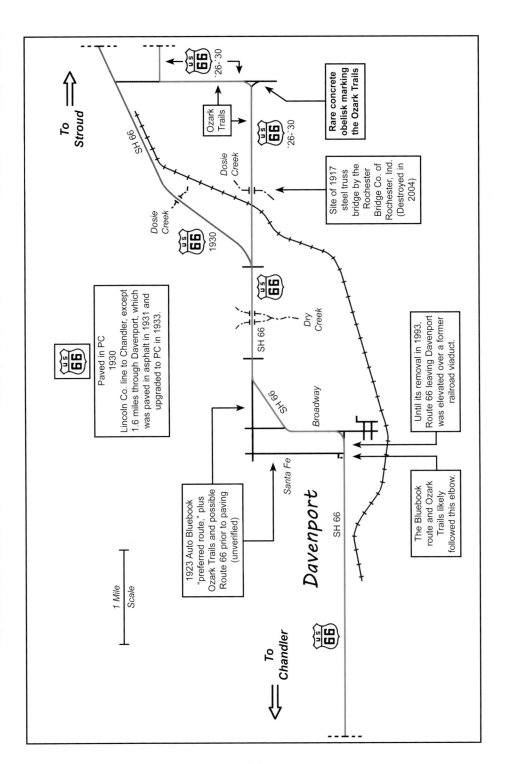

To
Stroud

US 66 '26-'30

Ozark Trails

US 66 '26-'30

**Rare concrete obelisk marking the Ozark Trails**

SH 66

Dosie Creek

Dosie Creek

US 66 1930

**Site of 1917 steel truss bridge by the Rochester Bridge Co. of Rochester, Ind. (Destroyed in 2004)**

Paved in PC 1930

Lincoln Co. line to Chandler, except 1.6 miles through Davenport, which was paved in asphalt in 1931 and upgraded to PC in 1933.

US 66 1930

US 66

SH 66

Dry Creek

SH 66

Broadway

1923 Auto Bluebook "preferred route," plus Ozark Trails and possible Route 66 prior to paving (unverified)

Santa Fe

Until its removal in 1993, Route 66 leaving Davenport was elevated over a former railroad viaduct.

The Bluebook route and Ozark Trails likely followed this elbow.

*Davenport*

SH 66

1 Mile
Scale

To
Chandler

US 66

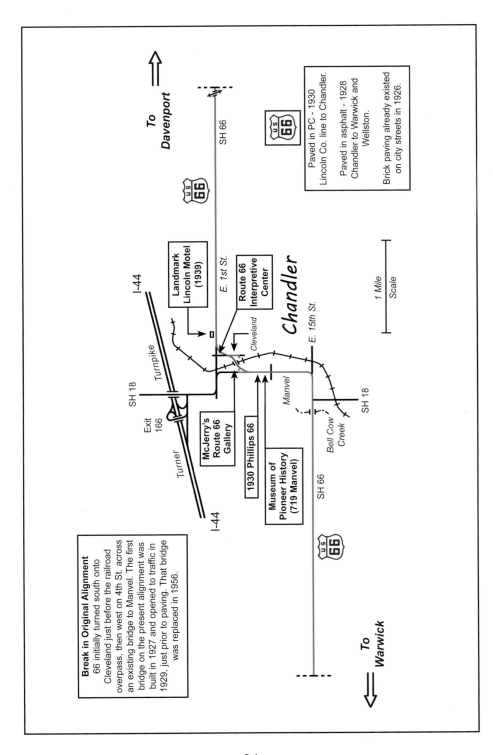

To
Davenport

SH 66

US 66

**Landmark
Lincoln Motel
(1939)**

E. 1st St.

**Route 66
Interpretive
Center**

Cleveland

*Chandler*

E. 15th St.

1 Mile
Scale

Paved in PC - 1930
Lincoln Co. line to Chandler.

Paved in asphalt - 1928
Chandler to Warwick and
Wellston.

Brick paving already existed
on city streets in 1926.

I-44

Turnpike

SH 18

Exit
166

Turner

I-44

**McJerry's
Route 66
Gallery**

**1930 Phillips 66**

**Museum of
Pioneer History
(719 Manvel)**

Manvel

SH 18

Bell Cow
Creek

SH 66

US 66

**Break in Original Alignment**
66 initially turned south onto
Cleveland just before the railroad
overpass, then west on 4th St. across
an existing bridge to Manvel. The first
bridge on the present alignment was
built in 1927 and opened to traffic in
1929, just prior to paving. That bridge
was replaced in 1956.

To
Warwick

*Early Chandler filling station, ca. 1930.*

*Jerry McClanahan collection*

The short distance between Davenport and the hillside city of Chandler offers a continuation of rolling landscape lightly decorated with meadows and sprinklings of trees as the highway continues its westward journey. Chandler, seat of Lincoln County and named for Assistant Secretary of the Interior George Chandler, opened its post office in September of 1891. Only six years later, virtually the

AT **CHANDLER**, FOLLOW THE CURVES THROUGH TOWN ON SH 66 AND PROCEED WESTWARD THROUGH **WARWICK** TO WELLSTON.

*Downtown Chandler in the 1940s.*
*Lincoln County Museum of Pioneer History*

*Chandler's WPA-built former National Guard Armory, abandoned for decades, has been beautifully restored and converted into a Route 66 Interpretive Center and a regional event venue thanks to local preservationists.*

*Shellee Graham photo*

entire town was destroyed by a tornado that killed fourteen citizens and knocked all but a few buildings flat. Instead of just moving on, however, the tenacious residents rebuilt, and soon enough the city thrived again.

Today, Chandler is a storehouse of Oklahoma history and vintage architecture, listing a dozen structures on the National Register of Historic Places. Route 66 icons include a WPA-built armory that now houses the Chandler Route 66 Interpretive Center and a Phillips 66 station built in 1930. Tucked within the row of stately old downtown buildings is the Museum of Pioneer History, one of the better locally supported museums anywhere in the state. Chandler is also the final resting place of local lawman Bill Tilghman, who was killed in what is considered to be the last of the Old West gunfights.

*This 1930 cottage-style Phillips 66 station still stands in Chandler (photo circa 1935 with unidentified attendants) at 7th and Manvel Ave.*
*Bill Fernau collection*

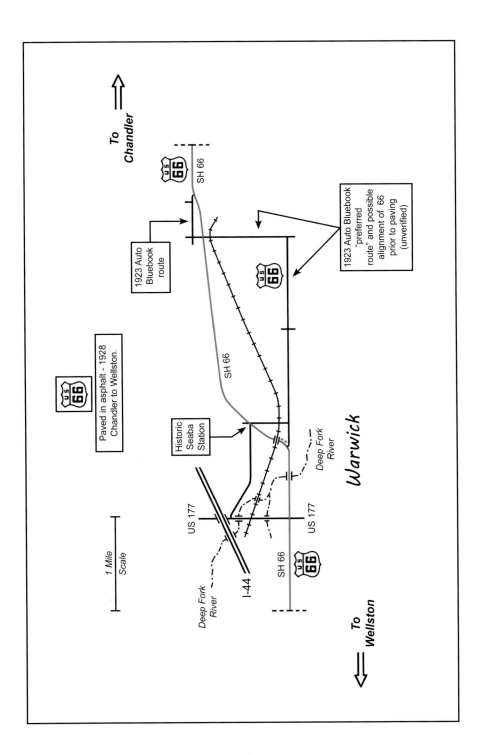

To
Chandler

SH 66

1923 Auto
Bluebook
route

1923 Auto Bluebook
"preferred
route" and possible
alignment of 66
prior to paving
(unverified)

Paved in asphalt - 1928
Chandler to Wellston.

SH 66

Historic
Seaba
Station

1 Mile
Scale

US 177

US 177

Deep Fork
River

Deep Fork
River

I-44

SH 66

*Warwick*

To
Wellston

97

Warwick Landmarks

Above: Historic Seaba Station

Below: Old pumps (now gone) in front of an abandoned grocery and station.

Not far from Chandler, on the slope of a hill, sits one of the few remaining Meramec Caverns barn ads still existing on Route 66 (easy to miss westbound as the sign also faces west). From there, the highway swings through Warwick, which was founded in the late 1800s and named for a county in England. One of the smaller burgs on the route, Warwick does have two notable landmarks—the former Seaba gas station, built in 1921, and the 1952 railroad trestle that straddles a graceful S-curve in the highway's path.

Next up is Wellston, which was also founded in the late 1800s near Captain Creek and named for resident merchant Christian T. Wells.

*The 1933 Captain Creek Bridge on SH 66B at Wellston.*

Here, Route 66 forks, with the original route turning northward into town on a three-mile jaunt (see map on next page), while the first paved alignment continues due west. Just before the turnoff, on the north side, an old, somewhat forlorn building marks the site of a early motor court called Pioneer Camp.

APPROACHING **WELLSTON**, SWING RIGHT ONTO SH 66B TO FOLLOW THE HISTORIC ROUTE THOUGH TOWN TO ITS RECONNECTION WITH SH 66,

OR,

STAY WITH SH 66 THROUGH **LUTHER** AND **ARCADIA** (SEE NEXT THREE MAPS).

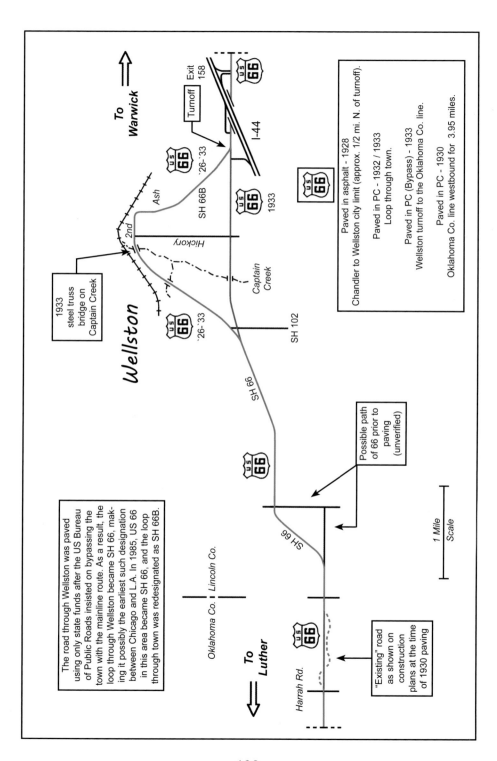

To **Warwick** ↑

Turnoff Exit 158

US 66

I-44

'26-'33

Ash

SH 66B

1933

US 66

1933 steel truss bridge on Captain Creek

2nd

Hickory

Captain Creek

US 66

*Wellston*

'26-'33

US 66

SH 102

SH 66

US 66

Paved in asphalt - 1928
Chandler to Wellston city limit (approx. 1/2 mi. N. of turnoff).

Paved in PC - 1932 / 1933
Loop through town.

Paved in PC (Bypass) - 1933
Wellston turnoff to the Oklahoma Co. line.

Paved in PC - 1930
Oklahoma Co. line westbound for 3.95 miles.

US 66

Possible path of 66 prior to paving (unverified)

99 HS

1 Mile
Scale

Oklahoma Co. : Lincoln Co.

The road through Wellston was paved using only state funds after the US Bureau of Public Roads insisted on bypassing the town with the mainline route. As a result, the loop through Wellston became SH 66, making it possibly the earliest such designation between Chicago and L.A. In 1985, US 66 in this area became SH 66, and the loop through town was redesignated as SH 66B.

To **Luther** ⇓

US 66

Harrah Rd.

"Existing" road as shown on construction plans at the time of 1930 paving

# — REST STOP —

## THE WELLSTON BYPASS

It was a bitter dispute, to be sure. The year was 1932, and the state of Oklahoma had reached an impasse with the US Bureau of Public Roads in the Bureau's demand that the paved alignment of Route 66 bypass downtown Wellston by almost a mile. At risk were federal highway dollars—all of them, and the choice facing the Oklahoma Highway Commission was anything but ambiguous. They could follow the Bureau's mandate, or else. It had come down to that. At stake, however, was much more than simply a preference for the path the road would follow. For several years earlier, as part of an irrevocable 1927 bond issue, the state had assured the citizens of Lincoln County that the highway would be threaded right through the heart of Wellston. And so they were stuck.

The US Government maintained that the bypass was cost-saving and efficient. The road from Chandler right up to the Wellston city limit had been paved in asphalt in 1928. Their plan for its continuation, however, was to proceed due west where the road curved northward toward town (see map next page).

In the end, state highway officials were reluctantly forced to pave the loop through town solely at state expense. There was no alternative. The state did not, however, suffer their losses without public comment. In what is possibly the first recorded instance of funds being withheld due to this type of disagreement, the commissioners had plenty to say in their Annual Report to the Governor for the years 1931-1932 regarding the BPR and the paving of US 66.

"Perhaps the most important accomplishment of the present Commission . . . was the closing of the gap at Wellston. This section was left unpaved for many years as a result of disagreements between the State and the Bureau of Public Roads. The gap is now being closed, as a result of the efforts of the present Commission. It is being done altogether with state funds."

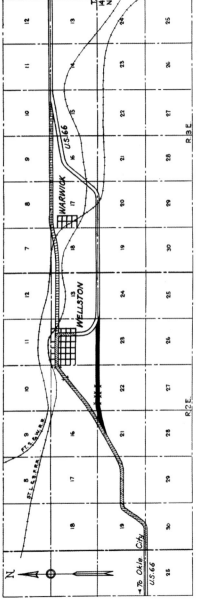

This sketch illustrates the situation on U. S. Highway No. 66 near Wellston, in Lincoln county, which the Bureau of Public Roads has made the subject of a controversy with the Oklahoma State Highway Commission. The road shown in diagonal lines from Wellston Southwest is now under construction, being paid for from state highway funds entirely. This is being built in strict conformity with the promise of the state to the people of Lincoln county at the time the bonds for the road were voted in 1927. The extension shown from Wellston to the point nearly 5 miles due east where it connects with the present Highway 66 shows the ultimate aim of the Commission. The present routing of 66, indicated by the white line, it will be seen, dips south, thence west and then north into Wellston. It will be noted that the eventual routing of the Highway, as planned by the Commission, will reduce future mileage construction and provide direct alignment for future traffic.

The section of 66, the elimination of which this plan eventually contemplates, is an obsolete type of construction. The roadway is only 18 feet in width. The wearing surface is of the black top type. It is constructed upon a five inch concrete base, which is without re-inforcements. There is evidence of serious base failure everywhere, and a general marked deterioration of the entire section. The life of this road, as estimated by engineers, will not be more than five years longer at best. Then complete replacement will be necessary. This is the factor taken into consideration by this Commission in the planning of the extension east from Wellston.

The heavy shaded section shows the paving demanded by the Bureau of Public Roads before it would agree to the release of our regular and emergency federal aid funds. The most casual observation of this situation shows how useless this section is to the completion of this Highway and the unjustified expenditure of funds that it involves.

102

In the same report, under a heading titled, "COMMISSION FORCED TO YIELD," remarks directed at the BPR were far less polite:

"Developments . . . in our relations with the road department of the Federal Government have served to emphasize its rigid, unrelenting and dictatorial attitude toward this State. As indicated by these developments, the judgment of the Bureau in local matters in which it sees fit to participate, is final and conclusive. Unless its will prevails, even to the minutest detail, it withholds the funds allotted to this State until such time as it literally forces obedience to its dictates."

In justifying their proposed routing of the highway, the commission included in the report a detailed map (opposite) illustrating the Bureau's plan versus their plan. The state contended that the road from Chandler to Wellston, paved in asphalt in 1928, would fail within another five years, and extending it (by way of the Bureau's bypass plan) was therefore a mistake. They proposed that, if the highway were paved through town, it would then be a simple matter to replace the soon-to-fail road with a separate, arrow-straight alignment extending back eastward from the center of the city. This road was never built.

How much of the state's argument was based on fact and how much was meant to dramatize the standoff or infer victimization is not known. What is known is that project records prior to 1940 in Lincoln County do not show any reconstruction on US 66 near Wellston due to road surface failure or otherwise.

In any event, while the State Highway Commission may have suffered a dose of humiliation, the citizens of Wellston were the real losers, as it became the first Oklahoma town removed from mainline traffic by a significant distance. The only consolation was the paving of the historic alignment by the state.

Interestingly, Wellston can lay claim to one other distinction. As a result of the bypass, the town loop became State Highway 66, the earliest such designation anywhere on the route. In 1985, when US 66 was decertified and redesignated as State Highway 66 in Lincoln County and elsewhere, the loop through Wellston was changed to SH 66 "B," and remains so to this day.

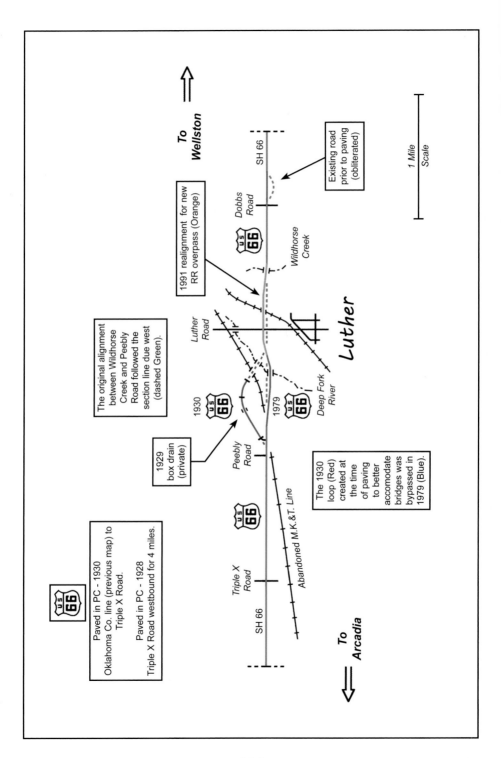

**To Wellston**

SH 66

Existing road prior to paving (obliterated)

1991 realignment for new RR overpass (Orange)

1 Mile
Scale

Dobbs Road

US 66

Wildhorse Creek

The original alignment between Wildhorse Creek and Peebly Road followed the section line due west (dashed Green).

Luther Road

**Luther**

1930

US 66

Deep Fork River

1979

US 66

1929 box drain (private)

Peebly Road

The 1930 loop (Red) created at the time of paving to better accomodate bridges was bypassed in 1979 (Blue).

US 66

Triple X Road

Abandoned M.K.&T. Line

US 66

Paved in PC - 1930
Oklahoma Co. line (previous map) to Triple X Road.

Paved in PC - 1928
Triple X Road westbound for 4 miles.

SH 66

**To Arcadia**

Following the historic route through Wellston leads to a 1933 steel truss bridge on Captain Creek. A twin of this bridge once existed downstream on the mainline route, but was destroyed in 2002. The remaining span owes its survival to the difference in traffic between the two alignments, though at this point all bridges of this type and age are endangered. Just west of the Captain Creek Bridge, a vintage concrete bridge has also gone the way of the wrecking ball.

*Above: Luther's water tower.*

*Above left: Old box drain on the historic loop just west of town (now on private property).*

From the point where the two alignments merge on the west side of Wellston, Route 66 sways and dips as it works its way across the hills toward Luther, following essentially the same path as it has since 1926.

Luther, which is just beyond Wildhorse Creek, sits on the south side of SH 66. The first town encountered in Oklahoma County opened its post office in 1898 and was named for Oklahoma City businessman Luther Jones. Points of interest here include a pecan grove on SH 66 at the junction with the town turnoff (Luther Rd.) and a winery a few miles north on the same road. Just before the Deep Fork River, concrete abutments that once elevated the old roadbed above the waterway and the nearby tracks of the former M.K.&T. Line still stand in testimony to the highway's original alignment. The remaining part of this historic loop is intact, and while it is not presently gated, is part of a private historical site. Its merging with SH 66 occurs just before Peebly Road, as shown on the map opposite.

Proceeding west from Luther, a historical marker describing the eastern boundary of the famous 1889 Land Run can be found on the left at the west end of the sharp S-curve where Indian Meridian Road intersects SH 66. And beyond the intersection with Choctaw Road is the site of a native stone structure on the right that once was a Conoco station. Though reduced to bare bones through the ravages

*Left:*
*The old station west of Luther during its operational days. Pictured are Lyle Melton and Red Abbott, ca. 1940.*

Arcadia Historical and Preservation Society

*Right:*
*The same station seven decades later.*

Shellee Graham

of time, it still makes for a good photo opportunity as the tour continues into the landmark-rich area of Arcadia (map opposite).

Just about one mile from the old station, SH 66 bends hard right to ascend a hill. This path follows an alignment that bypassed the historic route, which continues straight ahead at the curve as a weathered strip of Portland Concrete. Still driveable, this one-mile loop of original roadbed swings around the opposite side of the hill  and is distinguished in its own right, having been added to

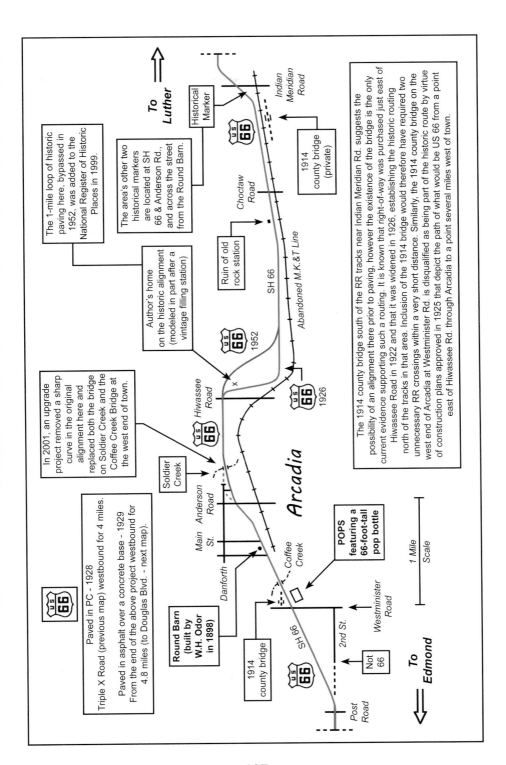

The 1-mile loop of historic paving here, bypassed in 1952, was added to the National Register of Historic Places in 1999.

The area's other two historical markers are located at SH 66 & Anderson Rd., and across the street from the Round Barn.

Author's home on the historic alignment (modeled in part after a vintage filling station).

In 2001, an upgrade project removed a sharp curve in the original alignment here and replaced both the bridge on Soldier Creek and the Coffee Creek Bridge at the west end of town.

Paved in PC - 1928
Triple X Road (previous map) westbound for 4 miles.

Paved in asphalt over a concrete base - 1929
From the end of the above project westbound for 4.8 miles. (to Douglas Blvd. - next map).

Round Barn (built by W.H. Odor in 1898)

POPS featuring a 66-foot-tall pop bottle

The 1914 county bridge south of the RR tracks near Indian Meridian Rd. suggests the possibility of an alignment there prior to paving, however the existence of the bridge is the only current evidence supporting such a routing. It is known that right-of-way was purchased just east of Hiwassee Road in 1922 and that it was widened in 1926, establishing the historic routing north of the tracks in that area. Inclusion of the 1914 bridge would therefore have required two unnecessary RR crossings within a very short distance. Similarly, the 1914 county bridge on the west end of Arcadia at Westminister Rd. is disqualified as being part of the historic route by virtue of construction plans approved in 1925 that depict the path of what would be US 66 from a point east of Hiwassee Rd. through Arcadia to a point several miles west of town.

To Luther

Historical Marker

Indian Meridian Road

US 66

1914 county bridge (private)

Choctaw Road

Ruin of old rock station

SH 66

Abandoned M.K.&T Line

US 66 1952

US 66 1926

Hiwassee Road

US 66

x

Soldier Creek

Anderson Road

Main St.

Arcadia

Danforth

Coffee Creek

1914 county bridge

SH 66

Round Barn

Not 66

2nd St.

Westminister Road

1 Mile

Scale

To Edmond

Post Road

US 66

SH 66

US 66

the National Register of Historic Places in 1999. Its uniqueness is found not in its age or condition (which is remarkably good), but in characteristics relating to the road surface itself, which involves two completely different designs that adjoin not far from its midpoint.

The first portion, completed in 1928, was built purely of Portland Concrete as part of Federal Aid Project 137-G. The second portion, which begins at the top of the hill and was part of Federal Aid Project 137-F, was completed in 1929 and was built of a two-inch asphalt driving surface over a five-inch concrete base with nine-inch concrete edges. While both types were common during the early years of paving US highways, the Portland Concrete design soon out-paced both the asphalt and concrete/asphalt combination road surfaces to become the material of choice and ultimately accounted for the majority of first-generaton paving statewide.

*Author's residence on the historic roadway (see photo opposite) was modeled in part after a 1930 Phillips 66 station in Chandler (see page 96).*

*Shellee Graham*

First built as a county road in 1922, the initial right-of-way on the "Arcadia Loop," oddly enough, was exactly 66 feet wide. In 1924, it became part of SH 7 (one of several new, numbered state routes that signaled the coming of the end for "named" roads such as the Ozark Trails). In 1926, the US 66 designation was added to SH 7, and in 1928, in preparation for paving, the right-of-way was expanded to a width of 80 feet.

At the point where the two road types meet there remains on the roadside a concrete Federal Aid Project (FAP) marker with in-laid brass shields containing data for the two projects. As for the road itself, other than some patching of holes, its dimensions and surface have retained their originality, quite a feat considering it has remained open to traffic since its construction.

This short loop of Mother Road, bypassed in favor of an improved grade in 1952, is rare for a number of reasons, but most notably because it contains the only unaltered, surviving specimen of combination asphalt/concrete road surface in Oklahoma built to standards and still in use. It is also the only remaining stretch of first-generation paving that includes the adjoining of two different surface types. Today, it stands as an important example of the road-building technology of the era.

The historic route rejoins SH 66 at the point where Hiwassee Road intersects. Just past Soldier Creek, at the junction with Anderson Road, there is another historical marker on the left, this one identifying the site where Washington Irving once camped.

The word "Arcadia" is said to mean "ideal rustic content-ment," which seems a good fit for

*Federal Aid Project marker describing construction of the historic roadway east of Arcadia.*

*Above: First-generation paving bypassed in 1952. East of Arcadia.*

this small, peaceful community founded in the late 1800s. In earlier times, cotton and agriculture were primary industries, but it was Route 66 traffic that assured its future. And survive it has, even after a 1924 fire destroyed half the town and the interstate highway system later stole away the flow of motorists it had come to depend on.

Today, Arcadia is home to several buildings listed on the National Register of Historic Places, including the landmark Round

*Right:*
*Arcadia's Round Barn as*
*it appeared in 1988*
*following collapse of the roof.*
Maxine Campbell

Arcadia Round Barn

*Left:*
*Fully restored, the*
*Round Barn*
*today is one of the*
*most visited attractions*
*on Route 66.*

Shellee Graham

*William F. Odor's barn in Arcadia, ca. 1900.*
*Arcadia Historical and Preservation Society*

ILENA LEWIS
MARCELLA KENNARD
COACH MR HUFF
DAISY BOGUE
HELEN NEKVAPIL

FRONT ROW
LUCILLE FENTER
DEA DOWELL
MARY FREED
ELLEN FENTER
DOROTHY SWEAT

ARCADIA HIGH SCHOOL GIRLS BASKETBALL TEAM
1928-1929

*Arcadia school photo taken the same year Route 66 was paved through town.*

*Arcadia Historical and Preservation Society*

Barn, which also boasts its own State historical marker.

Built in 1898 by resident William F. Odor, complete restoration of the barn began in 1989 following the collapse of the roof. Led by retired master carpenter Luke Robison, then in his seventies, the slumping structure was righted and then returned to its original condition by Robison and a group of local volunteers dubbed the "Over the Hill Gang." The job was finished three years later after extensive fund-raising and thousands of hours of sweat and muscle.

Originally constructed of locally harvested Burr Oak soaked in the nearby Deep Fork River for bending, Mr. Odor's barn dominated the landscape at 60 feet in diameter and 43 feet in height. During the renovation process, Robison and crew took great care to maintain the structure's architectural integrity, even soaking and bending the boards, just as William F. Odor had done nearly 100 years before. Now deceased, Luke Robison is considered a local hero.

*POPS in Arcadia became an "instant icon" as soon as it opened in 2007 and continues to draw tourists from around the world.*

Since opening to the public, the Round Barn has been operated by members of the Arcadia Historical and Preservation Society and has achieved great success, becoming one of the most publicized and visited icons anywhere on the route.

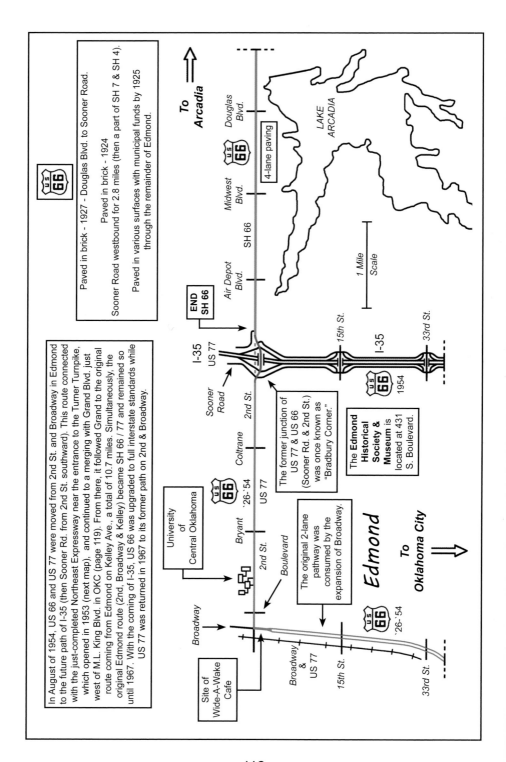

In August of 1954, US 66 and US 77 were moved from 2nd St. and Broadway in Edmond to the future path of I-35 (then Sooner Rd. from 2nd St. southward). This route connected with the just-completed Northeast Expressway near the entrance to the Turner Turnpike, which opened in 1953 (next map), and continued to a merging with Grand Blvd. just west of M.L. King Blvd. in OKC (page 119). From there, it followed Grand to the original route coming from Edmond on Kelley Ave., a total of 10.7 miles. Simultaneously, the original Edmond route (2nd, Broadway & Kelley) became SH 66 / 77 and remained so until 1967. With the coming of I-35, US 66 was upgraded to full interstate standards while US 77 was returned in 1967 to its former path on 2nd & Broadway.

Paved in brick - 1927 - Douglas Blvd. to Sooner Road.
Paved in brick - 1924
Sooner Road westbound for 2.8 miles (then a part of SH 7 & SH 4).
Paved in various surfaces with municipal funds by 1925 through the remainder of Edmond.

**US 66**

**To Arcadia**

Douglas Blvd.

*LAKE ARCADIA*

4-lane paving

Midwest Blvd.

**US 66**

SH 66

Air Depot Blvd.

1 Mile Scale

END SH 66

I-35 US 77

Sooner Road

2nd St.

Coltrane

The former junction of US 77 & US 66 (Sooner Rd. & 2nd St.) was once known as "Bradbury Corner."

15th St.

I-35

**US 66** 1954

33rd St.

The **Edmond Historical Society & Museum** is located at 431 S. Boulevard.

University of Central Oklahoma

**US 66** '26-'54 US 77

Bryant

2nd St.

Boulevard

The original 2-lane pathway was consumed by the expansion of Broadway.

*Edmond*

**To Oklahoma City**

Broadway

Site of Wide-A-Wake Cafe

Broadway & US 77

15th St.

**US 66** '26-'54

33rd St.

At the west edge of Arcadia, one of the route's newest icons cannot be missed. POPS, with its 66-foot-tall lighted pop bottle, a cafe, and over 500 brands of soda to choose from, opened in 2007 to virtual instant recognition and has since become an irresistible draw for roadies worldwide.

FROM ARCADIA, PROCEED WEST ON SH 66 TO **EDMOND**, CROSSING OVER I-35 AND ENTERING TOWN ON 2ND STREET. AT BROADWAY, TURN LEFT AND PROCEED SOUTH TO THE EXIT FOR KELLEY AVENUE (NEXT MAP).

*Right:*
*The intersection of today's I-35 and SH66 was once known as Bradbury Corner. The north-south highway then was US77 (now Sooner Road), which is a service road to the interstate. Photo Circa 1940s.*

*Oklahoma Department of Transportation*

*Left:*
*The not-so-glory days of traveling Route 66. Traffic between Arcadia and Edmond, 1950.*

*Oklahoma Department of Transportation*

Named for rancher Eddy B. Townsend, Edmond sprung up as a watering hole and shipping depot for the Santa Fe Railroad around 1887 and was settled during the historic land run of 1889. In August of that year, settlers built the first schoolhouse in Oklahoma Territory here, which has been restored and still stands at the intersection of 2nd Street (Route 66) and Boulevard. In 1891, the Territorial Normal School for higher education was established on the site that later became the campus of Central State College (now the University of Central Oklahoma). Just south of 2nd Street on Boulevard is the Edmond Historical Society Museum, which contains a permanent exhibit devoted to transportation and Route 66.

Now a major, upscale suburb of Oklahoma City, Edmond has

*Edmond's Camp Dixie, on Route 66 at 703 E. 2nd (now part of the UCO campus), was an early hybrid during the era when campgrounds evolved into motor courts. Postmarked in 1935, this card advertised cabins as well as a campground, and included a children's playground. Rates were $1.00 and up.*

*Card by E.C. Kropp Co., Milwaukee*

evolved from a quiet college town into a densely populated bedroom community with three high schools and a population well over 80,000. During its heyday, popular cafe stops in Edmond included the 66 Highway Cafe, Royce's, and the Wide-A-Wake. As a result of the rapid growth that began in the early 1970s, however, virtually no recognizable landmarks remain from the days when US 66 traffic flowed steadily along 2nd Street and Broadway.

Route 66 from Edmond to Oklahoma City originally followed

FROM THE KELLEY AVENUE OFF-RAMP MAKE A LEFT TURN, PASSING UNDER BROADWAY AND CONTINUE SOUTH INTO OKLAHOMA CITY.

*The Wide-A-Wake Cafe, ca. 1930s.*
*Picto Cards, Cincinnati. Author's collection*

114

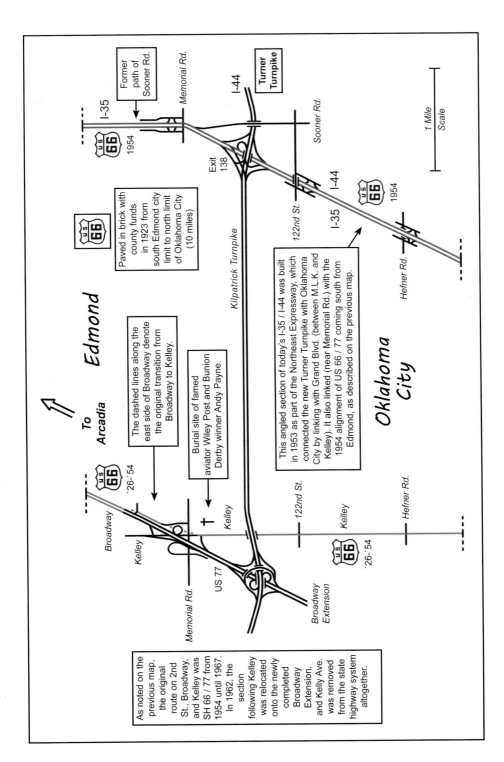

To Arcadia

To *Edmond*

*Oklahoma City*

Former path of Sooner Rd.

I-35

I-44

Memorial Rd.

Turner Turnpike

1954

US 66 1954

Paved in brick with county funds in 1923 from south Edmond city limit to north limit of Oklahoma City (10 miles)

US 66

Exit 138

I-44

I-35

US 66 1954

Sooner Rd.

122nd St.

Hefner Rd.

Kilpatrick Turnpike

This angled section of today's I-35 / I-44 was built in 1953 as part of the Northeast Expressway, which connected the new Turner Turnpike with Oklahoma City by linking with Grand Blvd. (between M.L.K. and Kelley). It also linked (near Memorial Rd.) with the 1954 alignment of US 66 / 77 coming south from Edmond, as described on the previous map.

The dashed lines along the east side of Broadway denote the original transition from Broadway to Kelley.

Burial site of famed aviator Wiley Post and Bunion Derby winner Andy Payne.

US 66 '26-'54

Broadway

Kelley

Memorial Rd.

US 77

Kelley

122nd St.

Kelley

Hefner Rd.

Broadway Extension

US 66 '26-'54

As noted on the previous map, the original route on 2nd St., Broadway, and Kelley was SH 66 / 77 from 1954 until 1967. In 1962, the section following Kelley was relocated onto the newly completed Broadway Extension, and Kelly Ave. was removed from the state highway system altogether.

1 Mile
Scale

*The junction of Britton Rd. and May Ave. on the Beltline Route, looking west, 1950.*

*Oklahoma Department of Transportation*

Kelley to Grand Blvd. (now I-44), as described in the driving directions (opposite). In 1931, a bypass or "Beltline" route was added, which provided the option of turning west just north of the city onto Britton Rd. from Kelley, then south on Western Ave. at the town of Britton to the mainline route at 39th St. This Beltline route was later extended westward along Britton Rd. to May Ave. (see maps on pages 118 & 119).

Britton, named for Santa Fe Railroad attorney Alexander Britton, opened a post office in 1889, the year of the land run. Though never on mainline Route 66, it was on the Beltline route from 1931 until 1953. Officially, that alignment was US 66 Alternate.

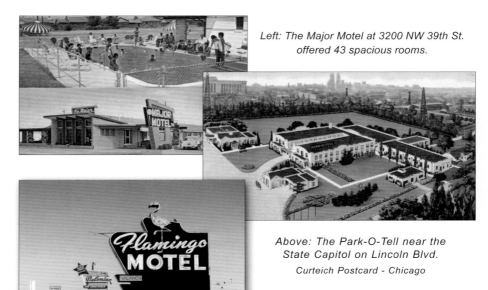

*Left: The Major Motel at 3200 NW 39th St. offered 43 spacious rooms.*

*Above: The Park-O-Tell near the State Capitol on Lincoln Blvd.*
*Curteich Postcard - Chicago*

*Left: The Flamingo, now gone, was once a prominent Lincoln Blvd. motel.*

116

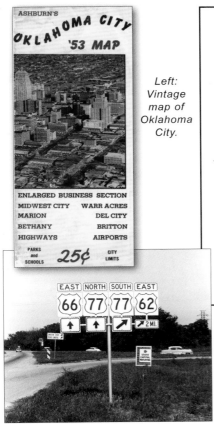

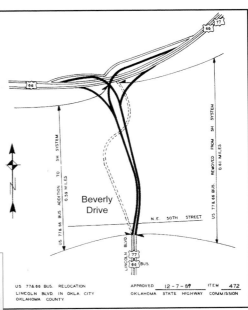

*Left: Vintage map of Oklahoma City.*

US 77&66 BUS. RELOCATION
LINCOLN BLVD. IN OKLA. CITY
OKLAHOMA COUNTY

APPROVED 12-7-59    ITEM 472
OKLAHOMA STATE HIGHWAY COMMISSION

*Left: Junction assembly at NE Exp. and Lincoln, looking east on NE Exp., ca. 1955, before construction of the 1959 interchange (above). Part of the realigned section of Lincoln (depicted with dashed lines on the document above), is today Beverly Drive.*

*Oklahoma Department of Transportation*

STAY WITH KELLEY TO THE JCT. WITH I-44 IN **OKLAHOMA CITY** AND TAKE THE WESTBOUND ON-RAMP, THEN EXIT IMMEDIATELY (RIGHT) ONTO THE LINCOLN BLVD. OFF-RAMP.

PROCEED SOUTH ON LINCOLN, MOVING TO THE RIGHT LANE NEAR THE STATE CAPITOL, THEN FOLLOW THE SIGNS LEADING FROM LINCOLN ONTO 23RD STREET WESTBOUND.

AT THE INTERSECTION WITH CLASSEN BLVD. TURN RIGHT ON THE HISTORIC ROUTE TO 39TH STREET, THEN LEFT ON 39TH ALL THE WAY TO A FORCED LEFT TURN AT FRANKFORD (WHERE 39TH BECOMES ONE-WAY). PROCEED ONE BLOCK TO 38TH, TURN RIGHT TO MAY AVENUE, THEN RIGHT AGAIN, MOVING IMMEDIATELY TO THE LEFT TURN LANE JUST BEFORE THE I-44 OVERPASS,
OR,
STAY WITH 23RD STREET WESTBOUND FROM CLASSEN TO MAY AVENUE AND TURN RIGHT, THEN MOVE TO THE LEFT TURN LANE JUST BEFORE THE I-44 OVERPASS.

AT THE I-44 OVERPASS, TAKE THE WESTBOUND ON-RAMP (LEFT TURN), WHICH CHANNELS TRAFFIC ONTO SH 66 AND SH 3 & 74. IGNORE THE RAMP FOR SH 3 & 74 AND FOLLOW SH 66 INTO WARR ACRES AND BETHANY, NOW ON 39TH EXPRESSWAY.

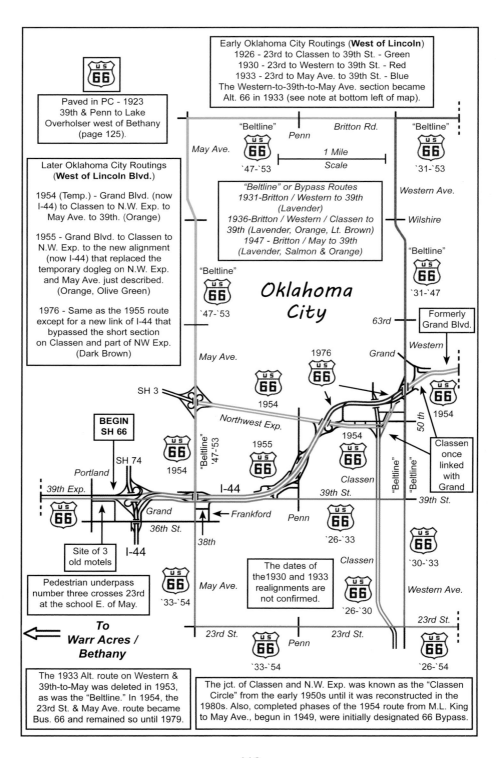

US 66

Early Oklahoma City Routings (**West of Lincoln**)
1926 - 23rd to Classen to 39th St. - Green
1930 - 23rd to Western to 39th St. - Red
1933 - 23rd to May Ave. to 39th St. - Blue
The Western-to-39th-to-May Ave. section became
Alt. 66 in 1933 (see note at bottom left of map).

Paved in PC - 1923
39th & Penn to Lake
Overholser west of Bethany
(page 125).

"Beltline"
US 66
Penn
Britton Rd.
"Beltline"
US 66

May Ave.
US 66
1 Mile
Scale
`31-`53

`47-`53

Later Oklahoma City Routings
(**West of Lincoln Blvd.**)

1954 (Temp.) - Grand Blvd. (now
I-44) to Classen to N.W. Exp. to
May Ave. to 39th. (Orange)

1955 - Grand Blvd. to Classen to
N.W. Exp. to the new alignment
(now I-44) that replaced the
temporary dogleg on N.W. Exp.
and May Ave. just described.
(Orange, Olive Green)

1976 - Same as the 1955 route
except for a new link of I-44 that
bypassed the short section
on Classen and part of NW Exp.
(Dark Brown)

"Beltline" or Bypass Routes
1931-Britton / Western to 39th
(Lavender)
1936-Britton / Western / Classen to
39th (Lavender, Orange, Lt. Brown)
1947 - Britton / May to 39th
(Lavender, Salmon & Orange)

Western Ave.

Wilshire

"Beltline"
US 66
`31-`47

"Beltline"
US 66
`47-`53

Oklahoma
City

63rd

Formerly
Grand Blvd.

Western

May Ave.

1976
US 66
Grand

SH 3

1954

Northwest Exp.

1954

50 th

1954

BEGIN
SH 66

US 66
`47-`53

1955
US 66

1954
US 66

Classen

"Beltline"

"Beltline"

Classen
once
linked
with
Grand

SH 74

Portland
1954

I-44
39th St.

39th St.

39th Exp.

US 66

Grand
36th St.
38th

Frankford
Penn

US 66
`26-`33

Site of 3
old motels

I-44

Pedestrian underpass
number three crosses 23rd
at the school E. of May.

US 66
`33-`54
May Ave.

The dates of
the 1930 and 1933
realignments are
not confirmed.

Classen
`30-`33

US 66
`26-`30
Western Ave.

**To
Warr Acres /
Bethany**

23rd St.
US 66
`33-`54
Penn

23rd St.
23rd St.
US 66
`26-`54

The 1933 Alt. route on Western &
39th-to-May was deleted in 1953,
as was the "Beltline." In 1954, the
23rd St. & May Ave. route became
Bus. 66 and remained so until 1979.

The jct. of Classen and N.W. Exp. was known as the "Classen
Circle" from the early 1950s until it was reconstructed in the
1980s. Also, completed phases of the 1954 route from M.L. King
to May Ave., begun in 1949, were initially designated 66 Bypass.

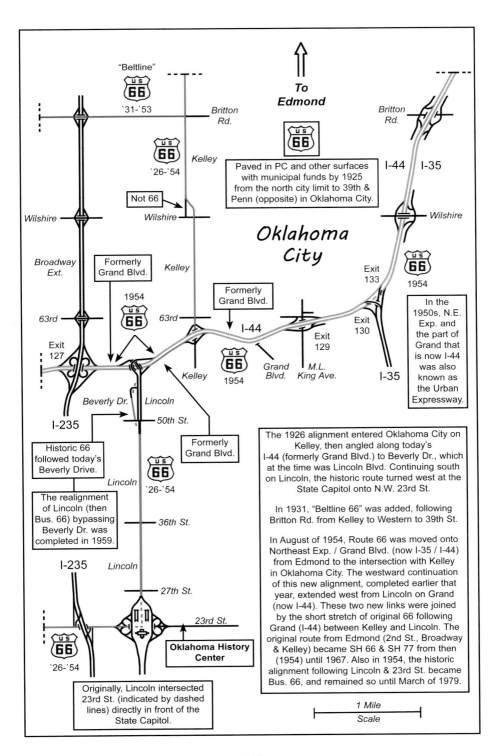

Oklahoma City, the state's largest municipality and the seat of Oklahoma County, replaced Guthrie as the State Capitol in 1910, three years after statehood. The first post office was established here on December 30, 1887.

Like other metropolitan areas through which Route 66 passes, much of the architecture here has fallen victim to the passage of time or to progress. Lincoln Blvd., the Mother Road's gateway to the city, once was clogged with motels, but now is literally stripped bare. Still, a keen eye can spot plenty of reminders of the glory days throughout the city, particularly along the 23rd St., Classen, and N.W. 39th St. pathways.

*1950s postcard view shows an eastbound view of*
*Rt. 66 / NE Expressway (now I-44) at its intersection wtth Kelley Ave.*
*Baxtone - Amarillo, Texas*

Originally located almost on the Capitol's doorstep were two significant Lincoln Blvd. establishments—the Park-O-Tell tourist court, one of the earliest and largest of the strip's motor hotels (see image on page 116), and Beverly's Restaurant, known for its "Chicken in the Rough." In fact, it was Beverly's popular recipe for chicken that brought fame to its owner and made it a universally known Route 66 icon. The sites of both the Park-O-Tell and Beverly's are now occupied by government office buildings.

The owner of Beverly's and creator of "Chicken in the Rough," Beverly Osborne, is credited with developing one of the first food franchises in the US during the late 1930s. But it wasn't restaurants Beverly licensed, it was a menu item, one so popular that eating establishments all over the country paid for the right to serve it and to use Mr. Osborne's distinctive logo.

*The Cinema 66 Drive-In was sandwiched between Grand Blvd. and NE Exp. (66). The remains of the entrance on Grand Blvd. are now completely overgrown.*

"Chicken in the Rough" was simply one-half of a fried chicken, served with a small jug of honey and french fries (then shoestring potatoes). It was served without utensils, promoting the idea of eating chicken with one's fingers, a notion that caught on in a big way.

In addition to the original Lincoln Blvd. site, Beverly Osborne ultimately owned restaurants at a number of other Oklahoma City locations, including one at N.W. Exp. and Penn, which until 2008 still operated as Beverly's Pancake Corner. Osborne's home during this era was near Grand Blvd. on Lincoln, which was re-named Beverly Dr. in his honor following the reconstruction of north Lincoln in that area in 1959.

Just west of the Capitol on the 23rd St. alignment, and right around the corner from

*The Tower Theater's neon sign has been fully restored.*

*The Milk Bottle building on Classen Blvd. is one of Oklahoma City's best known icons on the original route.*

*Shellee Graham*

Beverly's was Dolores' Steak House, another popular restaurant frequented by the area's businessmen and politicians during the highway's busiest years. For lighter appetites and those in a rush, there was Cherry's for Hamburgers only a few blocks away.

Though much was lost when the capitol complex expanded, 23rd Street westbound from Lincoln overall has changed only

*Cherry's on 23rd St., where a malt was 10 cents and root beer a nickel, ca. 1949.*

*Archives & Manuscripts Division, Oklahoma Historical Society*
*Barney Hillerman collection*

moderately since the 1950s, and has recently undergone revitalization. At Classen Blvd., where the historic route turns back north, the "milk bottle" building there remains as a guiding landmark for Route 66 pilgrims.

Until the opening of the Turner Turnpike and the completion of the modernized 1954 mainline route, the Beltline saw considerable use. Originally coming south from Britton Rd. on Western Ave., it was later extended westward to May Ave., then turned south, as shown on the maps. This alignment, like the mainline, had its share of businesses as well as accidents and a regular need for upgrading and repairs.

*Beverly's Pancake Corner in Oklahoma City featured the last remaining Chicken-in-the-Rough neon sign on Route 66. In 2008 it was moved to their new location in NW Oklahoma City.*

*North view on May Ave. at 39th St. in OKC, 1953. This is the junction of the historic route, the upgrade route, and the Beltline route. (Map pg. 118)*

Oklahoma Department of Transportation

123

*Entering Warr Acres on the west side of Oklahoma City, the Carlyle, Nu-Homa, Starlite, and Arcadia motels once offered a variety of choices for motorists within the space of two blocks. Today only the Carlyle still operates as intended.*

The 39th St. leg of the historic route, like 23rd St., has managed to hold fast to a few gas station and old motel buildings, particularly between Pennsylvania and Portland Avenues.

*The 66 Bowl (1959-2010) lost its iconic sign when the building was sold.*

Shellee Graham

From a few blocks west of Penn to just west of May Ave., 39th was nudged slightly off its original pathway to make room for the 1955 4-lane alignment (later upgraded to I-44), and was wiped out where I-44 swings south at its junction with SH 74. On the east side of the interchange two former motels remain (note: 39th is still one-way eastbound here; to see these relics requires a detour south to 36th, west to Grand, and north to 39th). Just west of the interchange, where 39th resumes, a handful of old motels stand marooned like a short row of unsteady dominoes. Originally four in all—the Arcadia, Starlite, Nu-Homa, and Carlyle, the Starlite is gone and only the Carlyle still offers accommodations.

STAY WITH SH 66 / 39TH EXPRESSWAY THROUGH **WARR ACRES** AND **BETHANY**, THEN CONTINUE ON SH 66 TO YUKON, OR,
WEST OF COUNCIL RD., ACCESS THE HISTORIC ALIGNMENT ABOUT 1/2 MILE AFTER CROSSING THE RIVER BY TURNING LEFT AND THEN JOGGING RIGHT (THE 1924 OVERHOLSER LAKE BRIDGE IS NOW CLOSED). FOLLOW THE 1926 ROUTE ALONG THE LAKESHORE UNTIL IT CURVES STEADILY LEFT, THEN BEAR HARD RIGHT WHERE THE ROAD FORKS, PASS UNDERNEATH THE TURNPIKE, AND PROCEED WEST TO YUKON.

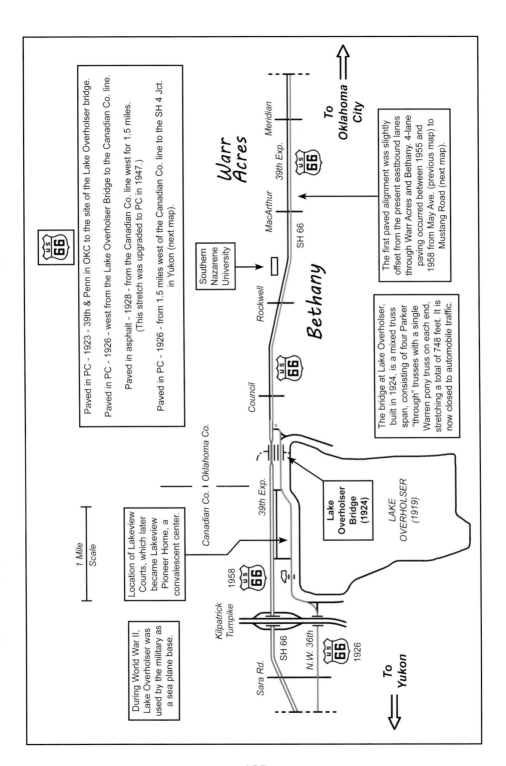

Paved in PC - 1923 - 39th & Penn in OKC to the site of the Lake Overholser bridge.

Paved in PC - 1926 - west from the Lake Overholser Bridge to the Canadian Co. line.

Paved in asphalt - 1928 - from the Canadian Co. line west for 1.5 miles.
(This stretch was upgraded to PC in 1947.)

Paved in PC - 1926 - from 1.5 miles west of the Canadian Co. line to the SH 4 Jct. in Yukon (next map).

The first paved alignment was slightly offset from the present eastbound lanes through Warr Acres and Bethany. 4-lane paving occurred between 1955 and 1958 from May Ave. (previous map) to Mustang Road (next map).

Southern Nazarene University

The bridge at Lake Overholser, built in 1924, is a mixed truss span, consisting of four Parker "through" trusses with a single Warren pony truss on each end, stretching a total of 748 feet. It is now closed to automobile traffic.

*Warr Acres*

*Bethany*

SH 66

39th Exp.

Meridian

MacArthur

Rockwell

Council

To Oklahoma City

Canadian Co. | Oklahoma Co.

1 Mile
Scale

Location of Lakeview Courts, which later became Lakeview Pioneer Home, a convalescent center.

During World War II, Lake Overholser was used by the military as a sea plane base.

Kilpatrick Turnpike

Sara Rd.

SH 66

N.W. 36th

1926

1958

39th Exp.

Lake Overholser Bridge (1924)

*LAKE OVERHOLSER (1919)*

To Yukon

It is entirely possible to drift right through Warr Acres and not know you have done so. Established in 1948 by real estate developer C.B. Warr, this mostly light commercial and residential community today merges unnoticeably with Oklahoma City on the east and with Bethany on the west. Route 66 here is congested with fast food joints, car lots, and assorted other businesses. Yet Warr Acres can claim one Mother Road distinction—the first state sanctioned Historic US 66 highway sign was installed here in 1990 at the corner of MacArthur Blvd. and 39th Expressway by the Oklahoma Department of Transportation.

*Route 66 through Bethany is a busy divided 4-lane today, but many of the buildings and shops retain their heyday character.*

Bordering Warr Acres is Bethany, founded in 1906 by the Nazarene Church and named for the Biblical village near Jerusalem. The Bethany-Peniel college, whose name was taken from the Peniel College of Peniel, Texas, moved its campus from Oklahoma City to Bethany in 1909, with a primary focus of training Nazarene ministers. Here, original town ordinances forbidding the sale or advertising of alcohol or tobacco and the presence of theaters remain in force, at least on 39th Expressway (Route 66), where the college, now Southern Nazarene University, is located.

Storefronts in Bethany's business district have retained a yesteryear flavor, and while its expansion to the south brought with it big city conveniences, Bethany has succeeded in maintaining a small town atmosphere.

Just west of town, Lake Overholser serves as one of the water supplies for the Oklahoma City metro. The classic "mixed, through

*The Lake Overholser Bridge, built in 1924.*

truss" bridge there, built in 1924, is one of only a few its size still in existence anywhere on Route 66. While not in imminent danger, it was closed for an extended period in the mid-1990s, only to be re-opened with a reduced load limit. Now owned by the City of Oklahoma City, it was closed once again in 2009, but left open to bicycles and pedestrians. Plans are to repair and ultimately re-open the bridge to light vehicle traffic.

*Located on the north shore of Lake Overholser, Lakeview Courts was an ideal overnight spot for heyday vacationers.*

*MWM, Aurora, MO.*

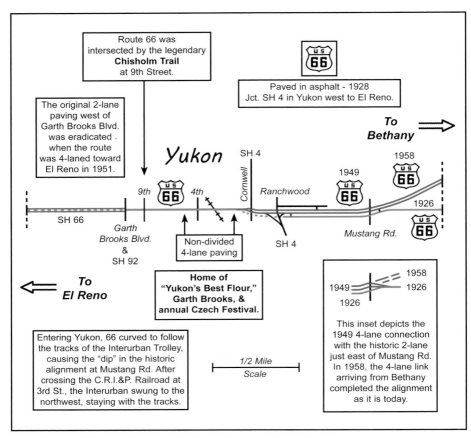

Route 66 was intersected by the legendary **Chisholm Trail** at 9th Street.

US 66

Paved in asphalt - 1928
Jct. SH 4 in Yukon west to El Reno.

The original 2-lane paving west of Garth Brooks Blvd. was eradicated when the route was 4-laned toward El Reno in 1951.

*Yukon*

SH 4

*To*
**Bethany**

1958

US 66

1949

US 66

Cornwell

9th    US 66    4th

Ranchwood

1926

SH 66

US 66

Garth
Brooks Blvd.
&
SH 92

Non-divided
4-lane paving

SH 4

Mustang Rd.

US 66

*To*
**El Reno**

**Home of
"Yukon's Best Flour,"
Garth Brooks, &
annual Czech Festival.**

1958
1949    1926
1926

This inset depicts the 1949 4-lane connection with the historic 2-lane just east of Mustang Rd. In 1958, the 4-lane link arriving from Bethany completed the alignment as it is today.

Entering Yukon, 66 curved to follow the tracks of the Interurban Trolley, causing the "dip" in the historic alignment at Mustang Rd. After crossing the C.R.I.&P. Railroad at 3rd St., the Interurban swung to the northwest, staying with the tracks.

*1/2 Mile*
*Scale*

*1949 construction (detailed on inset map above), looking east on the historic route.*
*Oklahoma Department of Transportation*

*Looking east on 66 in Yukon, 1940s. In the photo at bottom of page, looking west, the same junction with SH 4 North to Piedmont is at the traffic light just beyond the Conoco station.*

*Oklahoma Department of Transportation*

The prominent bank of grain elevators announcing "YUKON'S BEST FLOUR" leaves motorists little doubt as to their whereabouts. Founded in 1891 and located where Route 66 crosses the eastern fork of the famed Chisholm Trail, the town was named for Alaska's Yukon River by the Spencer brothers, who owned land at the site. Known for its annual Czech Festival, Yukon is also the home of recording legend Garth Brooks.

IF ENTERING **YUKON** ON THE HISTORIC ALIGNMENT, RECONNECT TO SH 66 AT THE INTERSECTION WITH MUSTANG ROAD. TO BEST ACCOMPLISH THIS, TURN RIGHT, CROSS THE 4-LANE, TURN AROUND, AND THEN TURN RIGHT ON SH 66 TO RESUME.

*Route 66 through Yukon today.*

*Banner: one of the more low profile links in the chain of Oklahoma Route 66 communities.*

Today there are no city limit signs and there is no operating post office, but Banner is still an active agricultural center five miles west of Yukon where Purcell Creek sneaks under the old highway. Known originally as Cereal, the town's name was changed to Banner (after the Banner School nearby) in 1911. Its post office closed in 1954.

FROM YUKON, STAY WITH SH 66 PAST **BANNER** TO EL RENO.

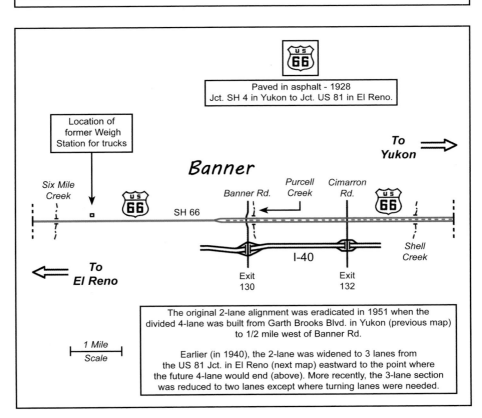

US 66

Paved in asphalt - 1928
Jct. SH 4 in Yukon to Jct. US 81 in El Reno.

Location of former Weigh Station for trucks

To Yukon →

# Banner

Six Mile Creek

US 66

SH 66

Banner Rd.

Purcell Creek

Cimarron Rd.

US 66

Shell Creek

I-40

← To El Reno

Exit 130

Exit 132

1 Mile Scale

The original 2-lane alignment was eradicated in 1951 when the divided 4-lane was built from Garth Brooks Blvd. in Yukon (previous map) to 1/2 mile west of Banner Rd.

Earlier (in 1940), the 2-lane was widened to 3 lanes from the US 81 Jct. in El Reno (next map) eastward to the point where the future 4-lane would end (above). More recently, the 3-lane section was reduced to two lanes except where turning lanes were needed.

130

El Reno is not only the seat of Canadian County, it is headquarters of the Cheyenne-Arapaho Tribe. Founded near the south bank of the North Canadian River in June of 1889, shortly after the April 22, 1889 Land Run, its name was taken from nearby Fort Reno, originally a cavalry outpost that later was an internment camp for WW II German prisoners. Today Fort Reno is an agricultural research center.

The name El Reno was chosen as a way for the town to distinguish itself from Reno City, which had taken root on the other side of the river the same day as the Run. Reno City, however, soon experienced an exodus when its citizens learned that the

GRACE'S MUSEUM AND CURIOS
2101 SUNSET     Watch for Stage Coach West Side of El Reno     (Highway 66) EL RENO, OKLAHOMA

*When it came to attracting Mother Road tourists, there were few limits, evidenced by the two-headed calf and double-bodied lamb once displayed at Grace's in El Reno.*
Author's collection

131

FROM THE JUNCTION WITH US 81 (SHEPARD) IN **EL RENO**, TO TAKE THE HISTORIC ROUTE TURN RIGHT ON SHEPARD, LEFT AT ELM (BORDERS THE CEMETERY), RIGHT ON HOFF (JUST PAST THE OLD RAILROAD TRESTLE), LEFT ON WADE, RIGHT ON CHOCTAW, AND LEFT ON SUNSET,
OR,
CONTINUE WEST AT THE INTERSECTION WITH SHEPARD ON US 81 / ROCK ISLAND / BUS. 40 TO WADE, THEN TURN LEFT ON WADE, RIGHT ON CHOCTAW, AND LEFT ON SUNSET, FOLLOWING THE BUS. 40 SIGNS.

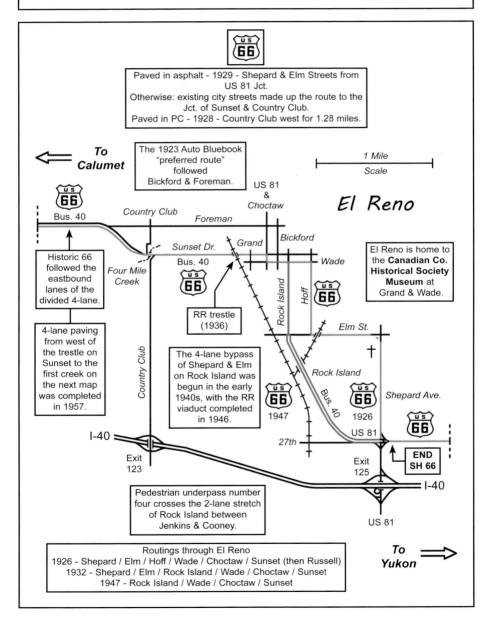

US 66

Paved in asphalt - 1929 - Shepard & Elm Streets from US 81 Jct.
Otherwise: existing city streets made up the route to the Jct. of Sunset & Country Club.
Paved in PC - 1928 - Country Club west for 1.28 miles.

To Calumet

The 1923 Auto Bluebook "preferred route" followed Bickford & Foreman.

1 Mile
Scale

US 66
Bus. 40

Country Club

Foreman

US 81 & Choctaw

El Reno

Historic 66 followed the eastbound lanes of the divided 4-lane.

Four Mile Creek

Sunset Dr.

Grand

Bickford

Bus. 40

US 66

Wade

El Reno is home to the **Canadian Co. Historical Society Museum** at Grand & Wade.

RR trestle (1936)

Rock Island

Hoff

US 66

4-lane paving from west of the trestle on Sunset to the first creek on the next map was completed in 1957.

Country Club

The 4-lane bypass of Shepard & Elm on Rock Island was begun in the early 1940s, with the RR viaduct completed in 1946.

Elm St.

Rock Island

US 66
1947

US 66
1926

Bus. 40

Shepard Ave.

US 66

I-40

27th

US 81

END SH 66

Exit 123

Exit 125

I-40

Pedestrian underpass number four crosses the 2-lane stretch of Rock Island between Jenkins & Cooney.

US 81

To Yukon

Routings through El Reno
1926 - Shepard / Elm / Hoff / Wade / Choctaw / Sunset (then Russell)
1932 - Shepard / Elm / Rock Island / Wade / Choctaw / Sunset
1947 - Rock Island / Wade / Choctaw / Sunset

Rock Island Railroad had been redirected to connect with El Reno rather than Reno City. It is also here that the western fork of the Chisholm Trail intersects Route 66.

Originally passing through a residential section where many stately homes still stand, US 66 was re-routed through El Reno more than once. Noteworthy among Route 66 points of interest here are the Ranger Motel, on the left just off Rock Island west of Shepard, and the old railroad trestles on Elm and Sunset. In the business district, good eats can be had at Robert's Grill (Wade and Bickford), and Sid's Diner (Wade and Choctaw).

On the west side of El Reno, a few more motels hang on, each in its own stage of

*Above:*
*Westbound view of the Rock Island viaduct in El Reno.*

*Right:*
*1929 map showing the historic alignment following Shepard, Elm, Hoff, Wade, Choctaw, and Russell (now Sunset).*
Oklahoma Department of Transportation

*West of El Reno, on one of the longest surviving stretches of first generation paving still in existence, date-stamped bridges testify to the structure's age and the vintage of the roadway.*

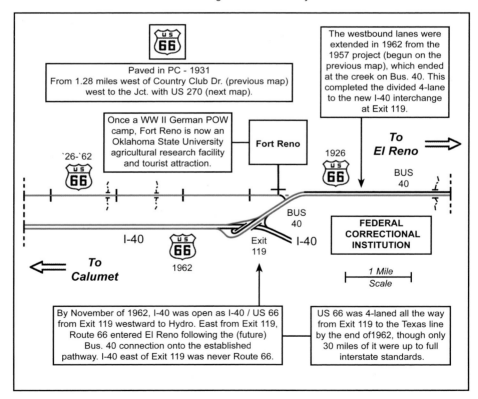

The westbound lanes were extended in 1962 from the 1957 project (begun on the previous map), which ended at the creek on Bus. 40. This completed the divided 4-lane to the new I-40 interchange at Exit 119.

Paved in PC - 1931
From 1.28 miles west of Country Club Dr. (previous map) west to the Jct. with US 270 (next map).

Once a WW II German POW camp, Fort Reno is now an Oklahoma State University agricultural research facility and tourist attraction.

Fort Reno

'26-'62

To El Reno

1926

BUS 40

To Calumet

I-40

1962

Exit 119

I-40

BUS 40

FEDERAL CORRECTIONAL INSTITUTION

1 Mile
Scale

By November of 1962, I-40 was open as I-40 / US 66 from Exit 119 westward to Hydro. East from Exit 119, Route 66 entered El Reno following the (future) Bus. 40 connection onto the established pathway. I-40 east of Exit 119 was never Route 66.

US 66 was 4-laned all the way from Exit 119 to the Texas line by the end of 1962, though only 30 miles of it were up to full interstate standards.

decay, while the Federal Correctional Institution remains entrenched, as it has since its construction in the 1930s. Signs in the area warn that "HITCHHIKERS MAY BE ESCAPING INMATES."

West of the prison, as the 4-lane curves on its approach to I-40, the historic route continues due west at the Fort Reno turnoff. Four and a half miles farther on, at the four-way stop with US 270, the 1933 bypass of Calumet, Geary, and Bridgeport begins. Here, the original alignment curled north to Calumet, west to Geary, then southwest to Bridgeport. That routing, however, was relatively short-lived (see "Rest Stop: The El Reno Cutoff," on page 145).

Calumet, founded in 1893, got its name from the French word "chalumet," meaning "shepherd's pipe." It was also the word Indians used for their ceremonial pipe. Though Calumet was on Route 66 only until 1933, it survived in spite of being bypassed, and today the town is a small but solid community still in business on the Mother Road's historic alignment.

To the west, the city of Geary was named for Indian scout Ed Geary (born of French ancestry as Edmund Charles Guerriere). A post office was established here in 1892. Being on Oklahoma's Postal Route, Geary residents had a strong interest in good roads and were responsible for bringing first the Ozark Trails and later Route 66 traffic to its doorstep. Although Route 66 never officially passed through Geary's business district, the Postal Route did, and US highway markers were reportedly once posted in a way that lured motorists right down Main Street.

---

BEYOND THE FEDERAL CORRECTIONAL INSTITUTION, WHERE THE 4-LANE CURVES TOWARD I-40, WATCH FOR A SIGN THAT SAYS: FORT RENO, NEXT RIGHT. MAKE THIS TURN ONTO THE OLD CONCRETE 2-LANE NEXT TO THE ENTRANCE TO FORT RENO AND CONTINUE WEST 4 1/2 MILES TO THE STOP SIGN AT US 270 (MAP ON PAGE 137).

TO STAY WITH THE BYPASS ALIGNMENT (FIRST PAVED ROUTE), PROCEED WEST FROM THE INTERSECTION FOR 7 MILES, TURN RIGHT ONTO THE 4-LANE, WHICH IS US 281 "SPUR" (MAP ON PAGE 136), THEN WATCH FOR THE LEFT TURN ONTO THE OLD 2-LANE AT THE TOP OF THE HILL AFTER 2 1/4 MILES (THIS TURN IS EASY TO MISS! SEE MAP ON PAGE 141). PROCEED DOWN THE LONG HILL TO THE T-INTERSECTION WITH US 281 AND TURN LEFT TO CROSS THE PONY BRIDGE ON THE SOUTH CANADIAN RIVER.

TO TAKE THE HISTORIC ROUTE FROM THE INTERSECTION WITH US 270, TURN RIGHT AT THE STOP SIGN AND FOLLOW US 270 THROUGH **CALUMET** AND WEST TO GEARY. AT THE JCT. WITH US 281 AT **GEARY**, UNLESS EXPLORING THE UNPAVED ROUTE TOWARD BRIDGEPORT (MAPS ON PAGE 140-141), TURN LEFT AND CONTINUE TO THE PONY BRIDGE, STAYING WITH US 281 BY TURNING RIGHT AT THE JCT. WITH US 281 "SPUR" (SEE MAP ON PAGE 141).

---

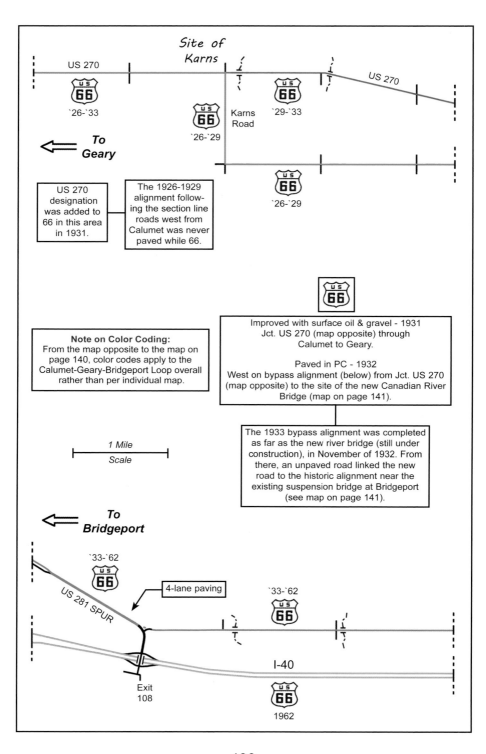

Site of Karns

US 270

`26-`33

To Geary

Karns Road

`26-`29

US 270

`29-`33

US 270

`26-`29

US 270 designation was added to 66 in this area in 1931.

The 1926-1929 alignment following the section line roads west from Calumet was never paved while 66.

**Note on Color Coding:**
From the map opposite to the map on page 140, color codes apply to the Calumet-Geary-Bridgeport Loop overall rather than per individual map.

Improved with surface oil & gravel - 1931
Jct. US 270 (map opposite) through Calumet to Geary.

Paved in PC - 1932
West on bypass alignment (below) from Jct. US 270 (map opposite) to the site of the new Canadian River Bridge (map on page 141).

The 1933 bypass alignment was completed as far as the new river bridge (still under construction), in November of 1932. From there, an unpaved road linked the new road to the historic alignment near the existing suspension bridge at Bridgeport (see map on page 141).

1 Mile
Scale

To Bridgeport

`33-`62

US 281 SPUR

4-lane paving

`33-`62

I-40

Exit 108

1962

136

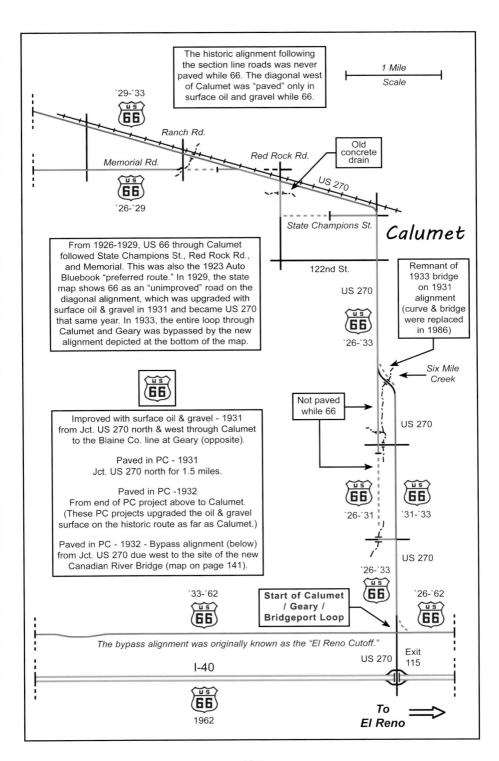

The historic alignment following the section line roads was never paved while 66. The diagonal west of Calumet was "paved" only in surface oil and gravel while 66.

1 Mile
Scale

'29-'33

US 66

Ranch Rd.

Memorial Rd.

Red Rock Rd.

Old concrete drain

US 270

US 66

'26-'29

State Champions St.

*Calumet*

From 1926-1929, US 66 through Calumet followed State Champions St., Red Rock Rd., and Memorial. This was also the 1923 Auto Bluebook "preferred route." In 1929, the state map shows 66 as an "unimproved" road on the diagonal alignment, which was upgraded with surface oil & gravel in 1931 and became US 270 that same year. In 1933, the entire loop through Calumet and Geary was bypassed by the new alignment depicted at the bottom of the map.

122nd St.

US 270

US 66

'26-'33

Remnant of 1933 bridge on 1931 alignment (curve & bridge were replaced in 1986)

Six Mile Creek

US 66

Not paved while 66

US 270

Improved with surface oil & gravel - 1931 from Jct. US 270 north & west through Calumet to the Blaine Co. line at Geary (opposite).

Paved in PC - 1931
Jct. US 270 north for 1.5 miles.

Paved in PC -1932
From end of PC project above to Calumet.
(These PC projects upgraded the oil & gravel surface on the historic route as far as Calumet.)

Paved in PC - 1932 - Bypass alignment (below) from Jct. US 270 due west to the site of the new Canadian River Bridge (map on page 141).

US 66
'26-'31

US 66
'31-'33

US 66
'26-'33

US 270

'33-'62

US 66

Start of Calumet / Geary / Bridgeport Loop

US 66
'26-'62

The bypass alignment was originally known as the "El Reno Cutoff."

I-40

US 270

Exit 115

US 66
1962

*To*
*El Reno*

137

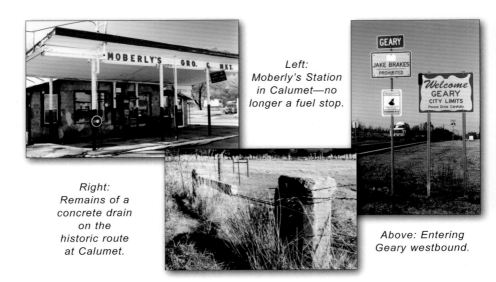

*Left: Moberly's Station in Calumet—no longer a fuel stop.*

*Right: Remains of a concrete drain on the historic route at Calumet.*

*Above: Entering Geary westbound.*

From Geary, the historic route angled southwesterly toward the river, first following a road built by the State Highway Commission in 1925 and then a road built by the town's citizens in 1917 in a bid for inclusion in the Ozark Trails. The two roads connect just south of the old railroad tracks where the former Postal Route turns west. Near the river, the highway swung to the right across Lumpmouth

*Westbound view where the four-lane project began near I-40 Exit 108.*

*Above: Trademark gutter on a "curbed" section of the 1932 bypass route west of El Reno—part of a 2-mile section destroyed (photo left) in 2000.*

Creek and tracked along the river to the old suspension bridge a mile north of Bridgeport (see facing page maps on pages 140-141). While the swinging bridge is long gone, the bridge pilings are not, and this alignment can still be driven as far as the river crossing in dry weather.

As the facing page maps on 136-137 indicate, the bypass route proceeded on a straight line all the way to I-40 Exit 108. From there, it took the path of least resistance to its

*Above: The 1932 bridge on Canyon View Creek west of El Reno (now gone), with inlaid brass Federal Aid Project marker containing project data.*

*Below: Gas station relic atop Bridgeport Hill (before remodeling by present owners) where the first paved 2-lane junctions with the newer 4-lane (US 281 "Spur"). See map on page 141.*

crossing of the South Canadian River. Approximately 2 miles of the first-generation paving on this alignment (beginning at I-40 Exit 108) has been replaced by 4-lane US 281 "Spur."

Prior to the reconstruction of Route 66 here, the stretch through these hills to the Pony bridge was arguably the most scenic anywhere in Oklahoma. Still pristine is Bridgeport Hill, which challenged early-day eastbound drivers with its steep grade and has delivered westbound motorists to the magnificent span on the Canadian River since the 1930s.

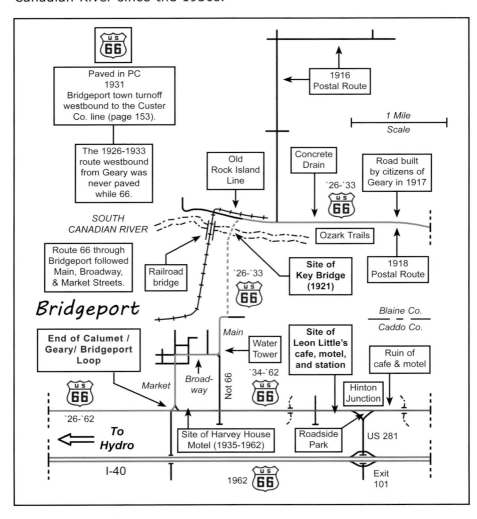

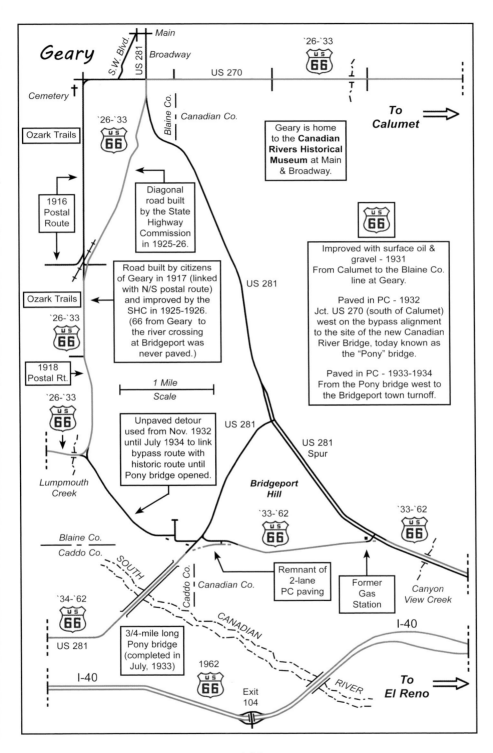

Geary

S.W. Blvd.

US 281

Main

Broadway

US 270

`26-`33
US 66

To
Calumet

Cemetery †

Blaine Co. | Canadian Co.

`26-`33
US 66

Ozark Trails

Geary is home
to the **Canadian
Rivers Historical
Museum** at Main
& Broadway.

US 66

1916
Postal
Route

Diagonal
road built
by the State
Highway
Commission
in 1925-26.

Improved with surface oil &
gravel - 1931
From Calumet to the Blaine Co.
line at Geary.

Paved in PC - 1932
Jct. US 270 (south of Calumet)
west on the bypass alignment
to the site of the new Canadian
River Bridge, today known as
the "Pony" bridge.

Paved in PC - 1933-1934
From the Pony bridge west to
the Bridgeport town turnoff.

Road built by citizens
of Geary in 1917 (linked
with N/S postal route)
and improved by the
SHC in 1925-1926.
(66 from Geary  to
the river crossing
at Bridgeport was
never paved.)

US 281

Ozark Trails

`26-`33
US 66

1918
Postal Rt.

1 Mile
Scale

`26-`33
US 66

Unpaved detour
used from Nov. 1932
until July 1934 to link
bypass route with
historic route until
Pony bridge opened.

US 281

US 281
Spur

**Bridgeport
Hill**

Lumpmouth
Creek

`33-`62
US 66

`33-`62
US 66

Blaine Co.
Caddo Co.

SOUTH

Caddo Co. | Canadian Co.

Remnant of
2-lane
PC paving

Former
Gas
Station

Canyon
View Creek

`34-`62
US 66

CANADIAN

I-40

US 281

3/4-mile long
Pony bridge
(completed in
July, 1933)

1962
US 66

Exit
104

RIVER

To
El Reno

I-40

Bridgeport Hill in 1946, looking west toward the Pony bridge (just visible in the distance). Oklahoma Department of Transportation

Today, the site of this unique river crossing is the beginning of the longest section of unaltered, first-generation paving still existing in Oklahoma, which stretches 18.3 miles from the end of the bridge's west approach all the way to Weatherford. While it is affectionately referred to as the "Pony" bridge, officially it is the William H. Murray bridge, named after Oklahoma Governor "Alfalfa Bill" Murray. Bridge plaques on each end of the span attest to its dedication and provide details related to its construction.

Not far from the bridge is the Hinton Junction, where US 281 turns off to the south and where cafes and motels once prospered. More than a

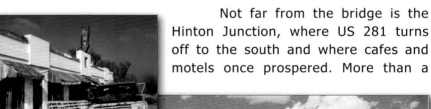

*The bridge on Lumpmouth Creek, once located where the original, unpaved route coming south from Geary swung to the west toward the Canadian River crossing, was replaced in the late 1990s.*

few of those forsaken businesses, which were strung along the straight stretch of road here, were owned by a man named Leon Little, who lived on-site next to the motel, cafe and station that he opened in 1934. Today, virtually nothing remains of his tourist empire.

Motoring west, Bridgeport's water tower soon comes into view to the north. At the town turnoff (where the bypass ends) is the site of the Harvey House Restaurant and Motel, which was owned and operated by Harvey Wornstaff from 1935 until 1962, the year traffic shifted to I-40. Leon Little's businesses ceased to operate about that time as well. Bridgeport, which had been bypassed in 1933, is today considered a genuine Oklahoma ghost town.

*Left: The uprights that once anchored the Key Bridge.*
Kathy Anderson

*Right & Below: Bridgeport's water tower and the former Harvey House Motel at the Bridgeport turnoff.*

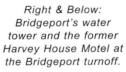

## THE EL RENO CUTOFF

It is said that progress is often painful. As it applies to Route 66, that axiom is especially true in regard to the paving of the highway in the early 1930s. Permanent surfacing was a top priority and, as it occurred, working its way piecemeal across the state, it brought with it adjustments in the alignment—some minor, some not so minor.

1932, without question, was "the" year for bad news in terms of communities taken completely off the route. Against

*The Key Bridge at Bridgeport, ca. 1930s.*
*Kathy Anderson collection*

the wishes of all concerned, Wellston was bypassed under mandate of the US Bureau of Public Roads. Farther west, it was decided as well to eliminate the circuitous route through Calumet, Geary and Bridgeport with a more direct alignment and a new crossing at the South Canadian River. This proposed bypass was to begin at a point west of El Reno and south of Calumet (where the highway made a 90-degree turn to the north), and end by re-linking with the historic route a half-mile south of Bridgeport. It was known as the "El Reno Cutoff."

From Geary, at the apex of the imperiled loop, the historic alignment led to the only reliable bridge within 50 miles. Known as the Key Bridge, it was truly a sight to behold. Constructed in 1921 about one mile north of Bridgeport, it stretched 1,000 feet across the river, 600 feet of which was in suspension. Hanging high above the current, it was guaranteed to never become a victim of the occasional raging waters that had destroyed every predecessor bridge dating back to the previous century.

Built by Oklahoma City businessman George Key, the swinging bridge at Bridgeport was not a free crossing, however. In fact, tolls ranged from 1 dollar for autos to 25 cents for a horse and rider. Even livestock were assessed 10 cents per head. The keeper of the Key Bridge, William "Whiskers" Phillips (who also supervised its construction), lived at the site with his family, where they operated the toll booth and where Mrs. Phillips sold sandwiches to hungry motorists.

In 1926, the Key Bridge became part of US 66, and in 1930 it was purchased by the state and turned into a free crossing. Increased traffic flow brought new prosperity to the three communities on the soon-to-be-bypassed loop, but unlike

*The Key Bridge toll station on the Geary side of the river, ca. 1923,*
*with railroad bridge in the background. Pictured L to R are: Mr. & Mrs.*
*W. L. Phillips, Mr. & Mrs. Bert Phillips, and their son Richard.*
Carol Duncan collection - Courtesy Oklahoma Route 66 Museum

Calumet and Geary, each of which were also on other US highways (US 270 and US 281 respectively), Bridgeport had by then come to rely on US 66 as its economic cornerstone. Ironically, the highway that brought so much promise to the little town on the Canadian was destined to be the cause of its starvation just seven years later.

Even so, it was the town of Geary that was primarily responsible for bringing the route to Bridgeport to begin with. The first known river bridge linking the two towns was built by the El Reno Bridge Company in 1894 to carry wagons. After that bridge and several of its successors were swept away by angry brown water, it was the citizens of Geary who turned serious about solving the problem. In 1917, they assembled their own road crew and succeeded in an effort to bring the northern branch of the Ozark Trails network to their area by building a new road from Geary to the river. They next solved the river crossing problem by initiating contact with George Key of the Postal Bridge Company to secure a permanent bridge there. In 1926, this route was chosen as the path of US 66.

In planning the El Reno Cutoff, a controlling factor was the decision to construct a replacement bridge over the South Canadian River three miles downstream (eastward) from the Key Bridge. The highway department boasted that this new span was to be "the most pretentious engineering project ever undertaken by the Oklahoma Highway Commission." Upon completion, it would be the longest bridge in Oklahoma at 3,994 feet (3/4 of a mile). The design selected called for 38 Warren pony trusses of 100 feet each on either side of a 25-foot roadway. Estimated cost of the project was $346,000.

Construction, which was awarded to the Kansas City Bridge Company, began in October of 1932, and was completed in July of 1933. Paving of the bypass from the junction of US 270 westward reached the new bridge in November of 1932. Paving from the Bridgeport turnoff (where the bypass ended) westward all the way to the Custer County line had been completed in 1931. This left an unpaved gap of less than three miles between the west end of the new bridge and the Bridgeport town turnoff.

Oddly enough, this short break in the route became plagued with delays, and would hamper completion of the overall bypass until the summer of 1934.

The culprit was a blend of funding holdups, other red tape, and weather. On May 4, 1933, *The Clinton Daily News*, under the headline, "BIG BRIDGE WILL STAND IDLE FOR SEVERAL MONTHS," reported that the earliest contracts could be awarded for the missing link was July. Construction would then take several more months. On May 18, 1933, the *El Reno American* reported that, "A gap of three miles of impassable country will render the span useless until the new roadway is constructed."

While the tone of many reports was somewhat critical, in truth, traffic was already flowing over most of the bypass route thanks to a short, unpaved, substitute road. This road linked the end of the bypass near the east approach to the new bridge with the historic route coming from Geary where it turned west at Lumpmouth Creek and shadowed the river to the Key Bridge.

By now it was being reported that the new bridge, "with the exception of the Municipal Bridge over the Mississippi River at East St. Louis, is the longest on the US Highway 66 between Chicago and Los Angeles." That, according to the August 14, 1933 issue of *The Clinton Daily News*. And while it had been named in honor of an Oklahoma Governor, because of the multitude of pony trusses from which it was built, it would eventually become known as the "Pony" bridge.

Contracts for the gap west of the bridge were finally awarded in September, and included funds to span a narrow canyon just east of the Hinton Junction containing tracks of the Rock Island Line. Completion of the entire project was now predicted for the following spring.

As the missing link west of the bridge was slowly closed, plans were made to celebrate, yet even the festivities were postponed more than once. According to published reports, the grand opening was first scheduled for April 1, 1934, then June 29th, then July 2nd. This last announcement was soon followed by a headline in *The Hinton Record* on June 20, 1934, that blared: "BRIDGE DEDICATION HAS BEEN POSTPONED INDEFINITELY."

The article explained that the paving was simply not finished. Finally, on June 26th, it was completed, needing only enough time for the concrete to cure before opening to traffic.

At last, on July 17, 1934, more than a year after its completion, the gala at the bridge took place, attracting a crowd estimated by some reports at 15,000. There was barbeque for all, a dance, and plenty of dignitaries on hand to make it official, including representatives from the National US Highway 66 Association.

Meanwhile, there was little to celebrate for the three

bypassed towns now permanently removed from the flow of US 66 traffic on the El Reno Cutoff. This was especially true at Bridgeport, where many of the city's residents soon decided to pull up stakes. Among them was Whiskers Phillips, former toll taker at the Key Bridge. He and his family did remain in the area, however, establishing a store and campground near the east approach to the modern bridge, which had been proudly declared by state officials to be the "gateway to all western Oklahoma travel."

The Key Bridge, essentially abandoned and used only for local traffic, was severely damaged by fire in 1946. In 1952, it was sold to a Kansas City salvage firm and promptly dismantled without ceremony. Only the rusty upright supports on each riverbank have survived the years.

Bridgeport, which was founded in 1895 and soon after became both a depot on the Rock Island Line and the site of the Postal Route's river crossing, progressed steadily and was the county's premiere town until the proliferation of motor cars caused its demise. Though still populated by a handful of residents and a scattering of barking dogs, the once booming town on the Canadian is today but a skeleton of its former self.

*Unidentified man at Bridgeport's Rock Island Depot, ca. 1930.*
*Once a regular railway stop, the tracks are now abandoned.*
*Kathy Anderson collection*

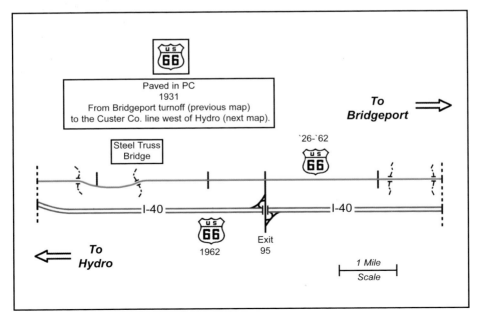

*This aging pony truss bridge (ca. 1930) spans a creek between Bridgeport and Hydro.*

The Canadian River valley has much to offer the Route 66 explorer, from the Pony bridge and Bridgeport itself to the ruins at the Hinton Junction and the ghostly relics at the site of the Key Bridge. Motoring west, the sense of being "lost in time" continues all the way to Hydro as the road meanders through rolling terrain a comfortable distance from the drone of I-40. The old pavement here, some with curbs and gutters, ferries traffic essentially the same as when first troweled to a smooth finish in the early 1930s.

Add to the mix a handful of both steel truss and concrete side-wall bridges, and it becomes a pure sampling of nearly every

US 66

Paved in PC
1931
From Bridgeport turnoff (previous map)
to the Custer Co. line west of Hydro (next map).

**To Bridgeport** ⟹

'26-'62

US 66

Steel Truss
Bridge

I-40

I-40

US 66

⟸ **To Hydro**

US 66
1962

Exit
95

1 Mile
Scale

ingredient that comprised the fabled route.

This trip through time comes to an end after about nine miles, as the interstate encroaches just east of Hydro until the two highways are running neck and neck and the legendary pavement becomes the north service road.

Founded in 1901, Hydro got its name, reasonably enough, from the area's vast supply of quality well water. Cruising the town requires a short jaunt across Deer Creek to the north of the route. Though the city's growth was no less stunted than many others with the introduction of the interstate, its proximity to I-40 and traffic on State Highway 58 has helped it retain its economic integrity.

*Grain elevators at Hydro.*

On Route 66 here, less than a half-mile west of the town turnoff, is the site of Lucille's, another of the best known and most photographed landmarks on the route. In many ways, the story of Lucille's characterizes mom and pop operations everywhere during the life of US 66, both in Oklahoma and beyond.

The station with living quarters overhead was built on the Mother Road's right-of-way here in 1927 by Carl Ditmore of Hydro. In the beginning it was known as Provine Station, named for the intersection next to the store. At one time, immediately west of Lucille's sat the Hilltop Cafe, and on the other side of US 66 was a

152

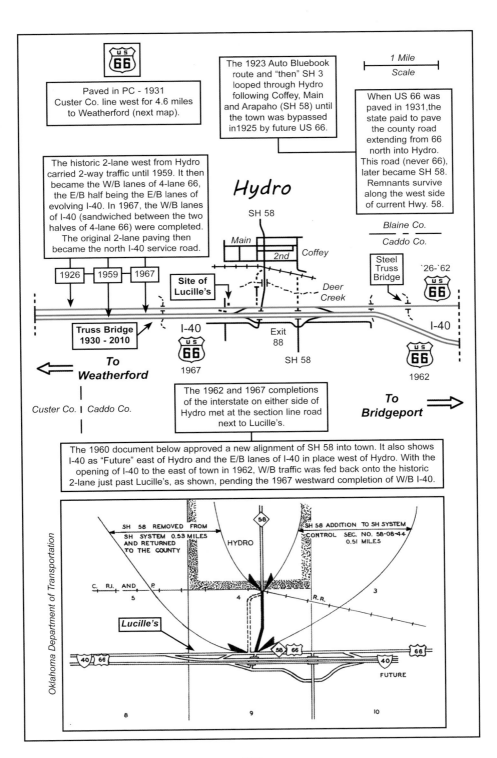

US 66

Paved in PC - 1931
Custer Co. line west for 4.6 miles
to Weatherford (next map).

The 1923 Auto Bluebook
route and "then" SH 3
looped through Hydro
following Coffey, Main
and Arapaho (SH 58) until
the town was bypassed
in 1925 by future US 66.

1 Mile
Scale

When US 66 was
paved in 1931,the
state paid to pave
the county road
extending from 66
north into Hydro.
This road (never 66),
later became SH 58.
Remnants survive
along the west side
of current Hwy. 58.

The historic 2-lane west from Hydro
carried 2-way traffic until 1959. It then
became the W/B lanes of 4-lane 66,
the E/B half being the E/B lanes of
evolving I-40. In 1967, the W/B lanes
of I-40 (sandwiched between the two
halves of 4-lane 66) were completed.
The original 2-lane paving then
became the north I-40 service road.

*Hydro*

SH 58

Main

2nd    Coffey

Blaine Co.

Caddo Co.

Steel
Truss
Bridge

`26-`62

US 66

Deer
Creek

1926  1959  1967

Site of
Lucille's

Truss Bridge
1930 - 2010

I-40

US 66

Exit
88

SH 58

I-40

US 66

**To
Weatherford**

1967

1962

Custer Co. | Caddo Co.

The 1962 and 1967 completions
of the interstate on either side of
Hydro met at the section line road
next to Lucille's.

**To
Bridgeport**

The 1960 document below approved a new alignment of SH 58 into town. It also shows
I-40 as "Future" east of Hydro and the E/B lanes of I-40 in place west of Hydro. With the
opening of I-40 to the east of town in 1962, W/B traffic was fed back onto the historic
2-lane just past Lucille's, as shown, pending the 1967 westward completion of W/B I-40.

*Oklahoma Department of Transportation*

SH 58 REMOVED FROM
SH SYSTEM 0.53 MILES
AND RETURNED
TO THE COUNTY

HYDRO

SH 58 ADDITION TO SH SYSTEM
CONTROL SEC. NO. 58-08-44
0.51 MILES

C. RI. AND P.

5

4

R.R.

3

Lucille's

40  66

58  66

58  66

66

40

FUTURE

8

9

10

Texaco station sitting on space now occupied by eastbound I-40.

Born in Illinois in 1915 as Lucille Arthurs, Lucille moved with her family to central Oklahoma as a child and graduated high school in Hinton in 1934. She married Carl Hamons of Hydro the same year and in 1941 they purchased Provine Station, taking over operation of both the store and adjacent motel units. The business was then re-named Hamons Court. Until her death 59 years later, Lucille would proudly call Route 66 home.

Lucille's, like other Route 66 landmarks, was a family business in the purest sense. One of Lucille's daughters, Cheryl, was born in

*Lucille with artist and Route 66 historian Jerry McClanahan at her store in Hydro.*
*1993*

the quarters over the station in 1948 and, along with her siblings, did her part by cleaning the motel units and waiting on customers.

As it was for other keepers of the highway, prosperity through the years was prone to ebb or flow with little warning. The war years were especially lean, and when the interstate arrived on their doorstep in the early 1960s times became tougher than ever. Hamons Court closed to tourists in 1962, the year I-40 opened east of town, and in 1971 Carl Hamons passed away. Ultimately, Lucille began selling beer in order to keep the doors open.

By then a fence separated the historic highway from the interstate and its wealth of traffic. To make matters worse, the westbound on-ramp diverted motorists onto I-40 just before they reached the station. Yet even then Lucille forged ahead, with never a thought to giving up or moving on.

Around 1974 the main sign blew down,  and she changed the station's name to Lucille's. Thereafter, the Hamons Court sign hung on the front of the locked motel units. Though the flow of customers was merely a fraction of what it once had been, Lucille persevered, accommodating the intermittent motorists who did stop in, without regard to the day of the week and despite her advancing age.

Ironically, decertification of US 66 in 1985 sparked its own resurgence. This in turn led to long overdue recognition of veteran business owners who had remained loyal to the highway over the decades. As a result, Lucille and others along Route 66 were now viewed as symbols of a lost cultural icon and were suddenly the focus of television producers, reporters, and tourists alike, all eager to learn of life on the highway and to hear stories of the road.

In 1997, Lucille's was placed on the National Register of

*Lucille's was a popular stopping point for tourists and car clubs alike. In this 1993 photo, Lucille plays hostess to the Oklahoma City Corvette Club.*

Historic Places. That same year, she published "Mother of the Mother Road," chronicling her 56 years on the route. In 1999, at age 84, Lucille was inducted into the Oklahoma Route 66 Hall of Fame.

Despite her failing health, the store remained open, right up until the day she died in August of 2000. In the minds of those who knew her, there was little doubt that Lucille would have continued greeting travelers until the end anyway, with or without the revival that established her as a Route 66 icon.

Following her funeral service, Lucille Hamons traveled the road she loved one last time as the procession motored up Route 66 from Weatherford to Hydro, stopping at the store long enough for a final farewell.

Only months later, the Hamons Court sign was acquired by Washington's Smithsonian Institution for a US 66 exhibit honoring transportation in America, which opened in 2003. Though Lucille is gone, the station remains as a testament to the thousands of entrepreneurs who spent their working lives on the roadside.

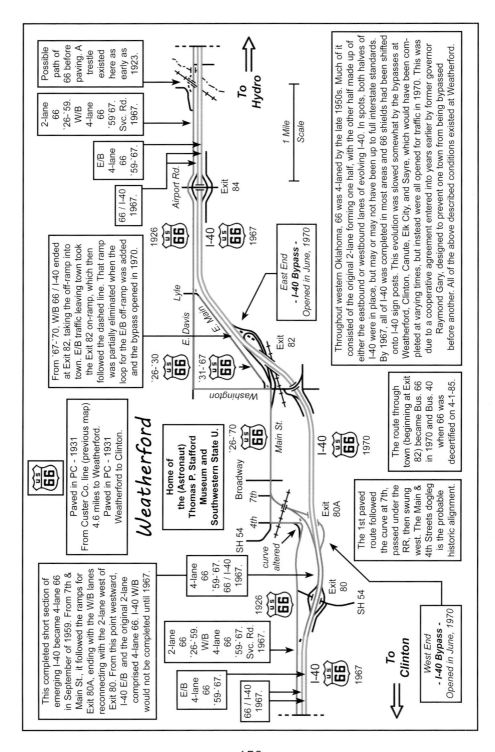

Possible path of 66 before paving. A trestle existed here as early as 1923.

2-lane 66 '26-'59. W/B 4-lane 66 '59-'67. Svc. Rd. 1967.

E/B 4-lane 66 '59-'67.

66 / I-40 1967.

To Hydro

1 Mile Scale

Airport Rd.

Exit 84

66 / I-40 1967

US 66 1926

I-40

US 66 1967

East End
- I-40 Bypass -
Opened in June, 1970

From '67-'70, W/B 66 / I-40 ended at Exit 82, taking the off-ramp into town. E/B traffic leaving town took the Exit 82 on-ramp, which then followed the dashed line. That ramp was partially eliminated when the loop for the E/B off-ramp was added and the bypass opened in 1970.

E. Davis    Lyle

'26-'30

US 66 '31-'67

E. Main

Exit 82

Washington

Throughout western Oklahoma, 66 was 4-laned by the late 1950s. Much of it consisted of the original 2-lane forming one half, with the other half made up of either the eastbound or westbound lanes of evolving I-40. In spots, both halves of I-40 were in place, but may or may not have been up to full interstate standards. By 1967, all of I-40 was completed in most areas and 66 shields had been shifted onto I-40 sign posts. This evolution was slowed somewhat by the bypasses at Weatherford, Clinton, Canute, Elk City, and Sayre, which would have been completed at varying times, but instead were all opened for traffic in 1970. This was due to a cooperative agreement entered into years earlier by former governor Raymond Gary, designed to prevent one town from being bypassed before another. All of the above described conditions existed at Weatherford.

Paved in PC - 1931
From Custer Co. line (previous map)
4.6 miles to Weatherford.
Paved in PC - 1931
Weatherford to Clinton.

*Weatherford*

**Home of
the (Astronaut)
Thomas P. Stafford
Museum and
Southwestern State U.**

US 66 '26-'70

Main St.

I-40

US 66 1970

The route through town (beginning at Exit 82) became Bus. 66 in 1970 and Bus. 40 when 66 was decertified on 4-1-85.

Broadway    7th

SH 54    4th

curve altered

Exit 80A

The 1st paved route followed the curve at 7th, then passed under the RR, then swung west. The Main & 4th Streets dogleg is the probable historic alignment.

This completed short section of emerging I-40 became 4-lane 66 in September of 1959. From 7th & Main St., it followed the ramps for Exit 80A, ending with the W/B lanes reconnecting with the 2-lane west of Exit 80. From this point westward, I-40 E/B and the original 2-lane comprised 4-lane 66. I-40 W/B would not be completed until 1967.

4-lane 66 '59-'67. 66 / I-40 1967.

US 66 1926

Exit 80

SH 54

2-lane 66 '26-'59. W/B 4-lane 66 '59-'67. Svc. Rd. 1967.

E/B 4-lane 66 '59-'67.

66 / I-40 1967.

I-40

US 66 1967

To
Clinton

West End
- I-40 Bypass -
Opened in June, 1970

156

FROM HYDRO, CONTINUE WEST ON THE SERVICE ROAD (ROUTE 66) TOWARD **WEATHERFORD**. AT THE STOP SIGN AT I-40 EXIT 84 (AIRPORT ROAD), STAY WITH THE NORTH SERVICE ROAD TO THE JUNCTION WITH E. MAIN / LYLE . HERE, FOR THE HISTORIC ROUTE, CONTINUE WEST (NOW ON E. DAVIS) TO WASHINGTON, TURN LEFT, THEN TURN RIGHT AT THE INTERSECTION WITH MAIN,
OR,
TURN LEFT AT THE INTERSECTION WITH E. MAIN / LYLE AND PARALLEL I-40 TO THE T-INTERSECTION AT WASHINGTON. TURN LEFT HERE, THEN IMMEDIATELY RIGHT TO ACCESS MAIN STREET WESTBOUND.

TWO BLOCKS BEYOND BROADWAY, MAIN ST. CURVES LEFT AT 7TH. CONTINUE DUE WEST HERE TO 4TH (SH 54), TURN LEFT, CROSS THE TRACKS, THEN CURVE RIGHT AND PROCEED PAST THE SH 54 TURNOFF TO STAY WITH THE SERVICE ROAD WESTWARD.

*Railroad trestle east of Weatherford with an angled passage to the right of the main span. The 1930 trestle may be an extension of an existing span (noted in 1923 "Bluebook") added to accommodate the 1931 paved alignment.*

Weatherford was founded in 1893 and named for Territorial US Marshal William J. Weatherford. Home to astronaut Thomas P. Stafford, it is also the location of Southwestern Oklahoma State University, known formerly as Southwestern State Teachers College.

Weatherford serves as the launching point for the many entanglements between early alignments of the highway and later routes that blended 4-lane projects with Interstate 40 (see map opposite). And while this interlacing continues all the way to the Texas line, it doesn't get any more complex than in Weatherford itself. Even so, the primary route though town, following Main Street, has changed little since the beginning, aside from a few modernized buildings. Here, many of the storefronts still adhere to their original facades, making it easy to visualize the town as it appeared several decades ago.

From Weatherford, after a straight run of approximately five

*Weatherford's Main Street, ca. 1959.*
*Postcard by Baxtone, Amarillo, TX. Author's collection*

*Weatherford's Bill's Motel is now in ruins.*
*Jerry McClanahan*

miles, the historic concrete changes to replacement asphalt where the road curves to the left. Here, the first paved alignment was cut by I-40 and can be seen resuming on the south side of the interstate. It is here also that the historic pathway continued due west, as depicted on both the map opposite and evidenced by the top photo on page 160. Most of this alignment can still be driven, though afterward doubling back is required to Exit 71 to reach the south side of I-40 and rejoin the path of the first paved route (refer to map).

FROM WEATHERFORD, STAY WITH THE NORTH SERVICE ROAD TO THE T-INTERSECTION, CROSS OVER I-40, AND RESUME WEST ON THE SOUTH SERVICE ROAD TO THE 2ND OPPORTUNITY TO CROSS BACK OVER, THEN FOLLOW THE NORTH SERVICE ROAD TO ITS CONNECTION WITH THE 4-LANE, WHICH IS BUS. 40 LEADING INTO CLINTON.

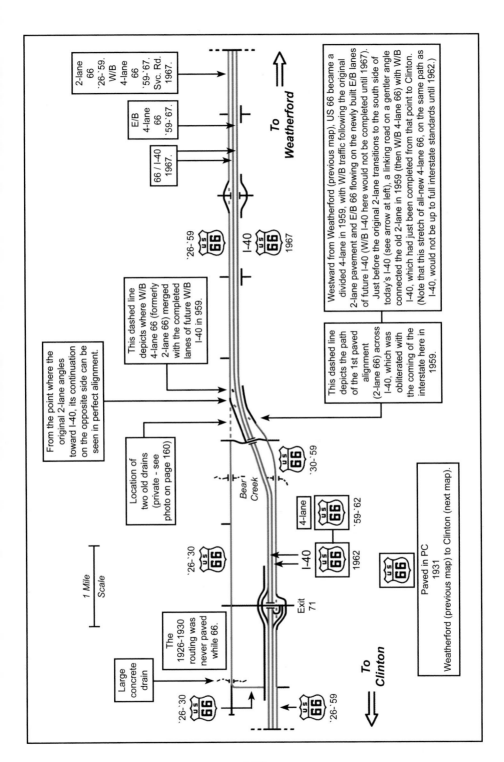

2-lane 66 '26-'59. W/B 4-lane 66 '59-'67. Svc. Rd. 1967.

E/B 4-lane 66 '59-'67.

66 / I-40 1967.

To *Weatherford*

'26-'59 US 66

I-40 US 66 1967

This dashed line depicts where W/B 4-lane 66 (formerly 2-lane 66) merged with the completed lanes of future W/B I-40 in 959.

From the point where the original 2-lane angles toward I-40, its continuation on the opposite side can be seen in perfect alignment.

Westward from Weatherford (previous map), US 66 became a divided 4-lane in 1959, with W/B traffic following the original 2-lane pavement and E/B 66 flowing on the newly built E/B lanes of future I-40 (W/B I-40 here would not be completed until 1967). Just before the original 2-lane transitions to the south side of today's I-40 (see arrow at left), a linking road on a gentler angle connected the old 2-lane in 1959 (then W/B 4-lane 66) with W/B I-40, which had just been completed from that point to Clinton. (Note that this stretch of all-new 4-lane 66, on the same path as I-40, would not be up to full interstate standards until 1962.)

This dashed line depicts the path of the 1st paved alignment (2-lane 66) across I-40, which was obliterated with the coming of the interstate here in 1959.

Location of two old drains (private - see photo on page 160)

*Bear Creek*

'30-'59 US 66

4-lane US 66 '59-'62

I-40 US 66 1962

1 Mile Scale

'26-'30 US 66

The 1926-1930 routing was never paved while 66.

Large concrete drain

'26-'30 US 66

Exit 71

Paved in PC 1931 Weatherford (previous map) to Clinton (next map).

US 66

To *Clinton*

'26-'59 US 66

*This drain, now on private property, was installed under the roadway in 1919 on the unpaved and future US 66 east of Clinton.*

Approaching Clinton, the north I-40 service road (Route 66) connects with Bus. 40. Once on the 4-lane, the fading path of the earlier 2-lane alignment tracks alongside the newer paving and through some trees before bending to follow the railroad and merge once again with the westbound lanes of the present roadway (as shown on the map on page 163). Once the road straightens out and makes its run toward

*Tables such as this one on the east side of Clinton (now on display at the Oklahoma Route 66 Museum there) were common along the roadside in the days when shade was a welcome sight and when picnic lunches were the rule.*

*In the western part of the state, I-40 cuts across the path of old 66 numerous times, occurring for the first time a few miles west of Weatherford. The second such instance is pictured here, just east of Clinton.*

the Washita River, a glance to the right on the approach to the bridge will reveal fragments of original Portland Concrete paving below the embankment of the present alignment. This original roadbed once crossed the river on the bridge pictured below.

Named for federal judge Clinton F. Erwin, Clinton was founded on the banks of the Washita River in 1903 when the Frisco Railroad arrived at the site. In 1932, the government established the State Tuberculosis Sanatorium here, which was a massive complex that contained dozens of buildings and consumed hundreds of acres.

Clinton today is the quintessential Route 66 town. Over the years, America's Main Street forged several different alignments along its city streets, creating a fertile ground for landmarks. The original route on Frisco is abundant with historic architecture, and on the final alignment (Business 40/Gary Blvd.), the Oklahoma

*The predecessor to today's river bridge at Clinton was angled, causing motorists to curve to the right coming off the bridge into town.*

*Oklahoma Department of Transportation*

161

ENTERING **CLINTON** ON GARY BLVD., TAKE THE HISTORIC ROUTE BY TURNING LEFT AT US 183 (4TH ST.) FOR ONE BLOCK, THEN RIGHT ON FRISCO AND LEFT AGAIN AT 10TH, OR,

FOR THE EARLY ALTERNATE ROUTE, TURN LEFT ON US 183 (4TH ST.) AND CONTINUE SOUTH TO OPAL, TURNING RIGHT THERE TO 10TH AND THEN LEFT ON 10TH, OR,

FOR THE FINAL ROUTE, CONTINUE ON GARY BLVD. ALL THE WAY THROUGH TOWN (THIS WILL REQUIRE DOUBLING BACK TO 10TH ST. TO RESUME ON THE HISTORIC ROUTE).

PROCEED SOUTH ON 10TH ST. TO THE "Y," THEN BEAR RIGHT PAST NEPTUNE PARK .

*Right:*
*Pop Hicks' Restaurant, lost to fire in 1999, opened in 1936 and ultimately became an institution on Route 66.*
*Postcard by Baxtone, Amarillo, TX.*
*Author's collection*

*Greetings from Clinton, Oklahoma*

*Left:*
*The Oklahoma Route 66 Museum at 2229 Gary Blvd. in Clinton is currently the only state operated museum devoted entirely to the Mother Road.*

Route 66 Museum is now ranked as one of the route's top tourist attractions. Just across the street from the museum, the Trade Winds Inn is known as an overnight stop for Elvis a number of times during the "King's" numerous car trips west from Memphis.

Among the many icons here, it was Pop Hicks' Restaurant, located next door to the Glancy Motel, that was the most recognized. For over 60 years, Pop Hicks served both locals and tourists with the kind of road food that exemplified the era of 2-lane America. Sadly, the last serving of hash was slung at Pop Hicks the day it burned to the ground in 1999, never to be rebuilt.

Aside from the numerous landmarks associated with Clinton, its greatest contribution to the highway came from two of its citizens, "Mr. & Mrs. 66," Jack and Gladys Cutberth. Jack, serving as Executive

162

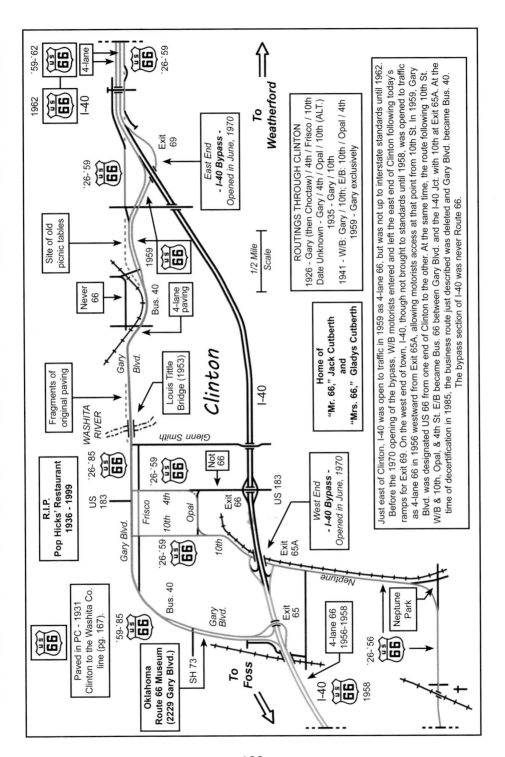

'59-'62    1962    I-40

**To Weatherford**

East End
- I-40 Bypass -
Opened in June, 1970

Exit 69

'26-'59

Site of old picnic tables

Never 66

1959

Bus. 40

4-lane paving

Fragments of original paving

Gary Blvd.

1/2 Mile Scale

WASHITA RIVER

Louis Tittle Bridge (1953)

**Clinton**

I-40

ROUTINGS THROUGH CLINTON
1926 - Gary (then Choctaw) / 4th / Frisco / 10th
Date Unknown - Gary / 4th / Opal / 10th (ALT.)
1935 - Gary / 10th
1941 - W/B: Gary / 10th; E/B: 10th / Opal / 4th
1959 - Gary exclusively

Glenn Smith

R.I.P.
Pop Hicks' Restaurant
1936 - 1999

'26-'85

US 183

Gary Blvd.

Frisco   10th   4th

'26-'59

Opal

Not 66

Exit 66

US 183

'26-'59

10th

West End
- I-40 Bypass -
Opened in June, 1970

Exit 65A

Neptune

Home of
"Mr. 66," Jack Cutberth
and
"Mrs. 66," Gladys Cutberth

Paved in PC - 1931
Clinton to the Washita Co.
line (pg. 167).

'59-'85

**Oklahoma
Route 66 Museum**
(2229 Gary Blvd.)

SH 73

Bus. 40

Gary Blvd.

Exit 65

**To Foss**

4-lane 66
1956-1958

I-40

1958

'26-'56

Neptune Park

Just east of Clinton, I-40 was open to traffic in 1959 as 4-lane 66, but was not up to interstate standards until 1962. Before the 1970 opening of the bypass, W/B motorists entered and left the east end of Clinton following today's ramps for Exit 69. On the west end of town, I-40, though not brought to standards until 1958, was opened to traffic as 4-lane 66 in 1956 westward from Exit 65A, allowing motorists access at that point from 10th St. In 1959, Gary Blvd. was designated US 66 from one end of Clinton to the other. At the same time, the route following 10th St. W/B & 10th, Opal, & 4th St. E/B became Bus. 66 between Gary Blvd. and the I-40 Jct. with 10th at Exit 65A. At the time of decertification in 1985, the business route just described was deleted and Gary Blvd. became Bus. 40. The bypass section of I-40 was never Route 66.

163

*The basement office of the Cutberth's Clinton home, from which Jack and Gladys, "Mr. & Mrs. 66," administered the business of the National US Highway 66 Association.*

WEST FROM CLINTON, PASS UNDER THE RAILROAD TRESTLE AND CONTINUE UNTIL THE ROUTE ONCE AGAIN PARALLELS I-40 (EXIT 62) AS THE SOUTH SERVICE ROAD. FIVE MILES FARTHER WEST, AT EXIT 57 (PAGE 167), TURN RIGHT, CROSS UNDER THE INTERSTATE, THEN TURN LEFT TO CONTINUE TO THE JUNCTION WITH SH 44 AT FOSS.

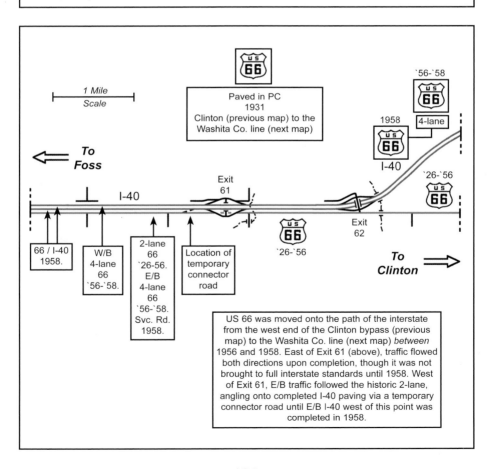

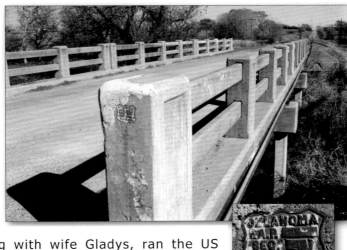

*This classic steel beam and concrete sidewall bridge west of Clinton is a near twin of the 1932 Canyon View Creek bridge on page 139. The attached FAP marker reveals its year of construction as 1929.*

Secretary, along with wife Gladys, ran the US Highway 66 Association from their home here for more than 20 years, distributing literature and otherwise working to lure motorists to the Mother Road. During the interstate's onslaught of the 1960s, the Cutberth's were at the forefront in the fight to prevent town bypasses, an effort that helped earn them their place in Route 66 history.

Leaving Clinton, the Mother Road swings right at the "Y," where a former roadhouse still stands. Just ahead on the left is Neptune Park, another make-work project of the WPA. Only a few miles farther on, I-40 reappears on the right at Exit 62. From here, the original Portland Concrete serves as the south service road until its path is once again cut by the interstate just east of Exit 57.

*The sticker on this '56 Olds 88 west of Clinton (now gone), was the work of the late Route 66 artist and icon Bob Waldmire. It's message: Repect Remains.*

165

*Foss: Not a ghost town.*

This is another point where the historic route and the first paved alignment part company. Originally, the highway continued due west here, across a bridge on Turkey Creek (abutments remain) to a left turn north of Foss on today's SH 44. The paved route bypassed this dogleg as well as the Postal route to the south of town to shadow the railroad (see map opposite).

Foss, named after J.M. Foss of Cordell, was founded around 1900. Demoted to ghost town status after the opening of the interstate, today the town has several operating businesses and many residents bringing new life to the area.

FROM THE INTERSECTION WITH SH 44 AT **FOSS**, CONTINUE WEST ON THE NORTH SIDE OF I-40.

*Sweeping curves like this one near Foss are a trademark of first-generation paving.*

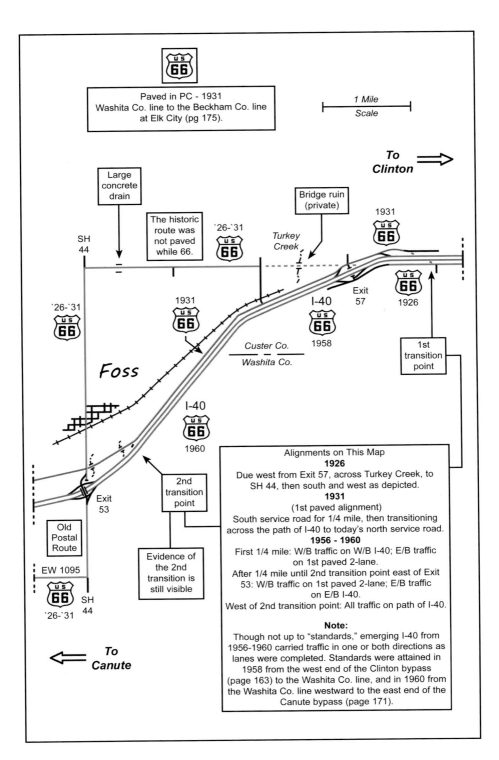

US 66

Paved in PC - 1931
Washita Co. line to the Beckham Co. line
at Elk City (pg 175).

1 Mile
Scale

To Clinton

Large concrete drain

Bridge ruin (private)

1931
US 66

The historic route was not paved while 66.

'26-'31
US 66

Turkey Creek

SH 44

'26-'31
US 66

1931
US 66

Exit 57

I-40
US 66

1926

Custer Co.
Washita Co.

1958

1st transition point

Foss

I-40
US 66

1960

2nd transition point

Exit 53

Old Postal Route

EW 1095

US 66
'26-'31

SH 44

Evidence of the 2nd transition is still visible

To Canute

**Alignments on This Map**
**1926**
Due west from Exit 57, across Turkey Creek, to
SH 44, then south and west as depicted.
**1931**
(1st paved alignment)
South service road for 1/4 mile, then transitioning
across the path of I-40 to today's north service road.
**1956 - 1960**
First 1/4 mile: W/B traffic on W/B I-40; E/B traffic
on 1st paved 2-lane.
After 1/4 mile until 2nd transition point east of Exit
53: W/B traffic on 1st paved 2-lane; E/B traffic
on E/B I-40.
West of 2nd transition point: All traffic on path of I-40.

**Note:**
Though not up to "standards," emerging I-40 from
1956-1960 carried traffic in one or both directions as
lanes were completed. Standards were attained in
1958 from the west end of the Clinton bypass
(page 163) to the Washita Co. line, and in 1960 from
the Washita Co. line westward to the east end of the
Canute bypass (page 171).

167

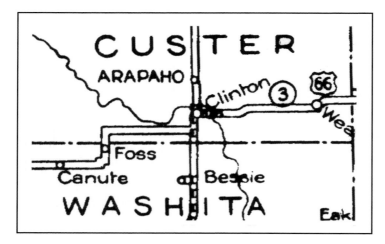

*Official 1928 map shows historic US 66 entering Foss from the north and following the section lines to the south of town, alignments modified when paving arrived in 1931. (See map opposite and on page 167.)*

Oklahoma Department of Transportation

AT THE FIRST INTERSTATE CROSSOVER WEST OF FOSS (EXIT 50), MOVE TO THE SOUTH SIDE OF I-40, TURN RIGHT, AND PROCEED TO THE NEXT INTERSTATE OVERPASS (ABOUT 1 1/2 MILES). CROSS TO THE NORTH SIDE OF I-40 HERE, THEN CONTINUE WEST ON THE SERVICE ROAD TO THE NEXT CROSSOVER (EXIT 47 - MAP ON PAGE 171). CROSS ONCE AGAIN TO THE SOUTH SIDE OF THE INTERSTATE HERE TO ENTER CANUTE.

*Rainbow west of Foss.*

The historic route from Foss followed the path of SH 44 south across I-40, then west at the first section line road for one mile, then south one-half mile, then west again toward Canute. This route junctions with the first paved alignment just south of Exit 50, as shown on the map opposite. Meanwhile, the first paved route from Foss transitioned from the north side of the interstate to the south side right through Exit 50. This pathway was once evident along a row of shade trees (now gone) that could be seen from the interstate overpass.

Soon after crossing paths with the historic alignment here, the first paved route swung back to the north side of I-40 to merge with the historic route just west of Clinton Lake. A short distance farther on, approaching Canute, the superslab cut through the path of Route 66 yet again. Overall, this stretch of road now requires several interstate hops within a relatively short distance.

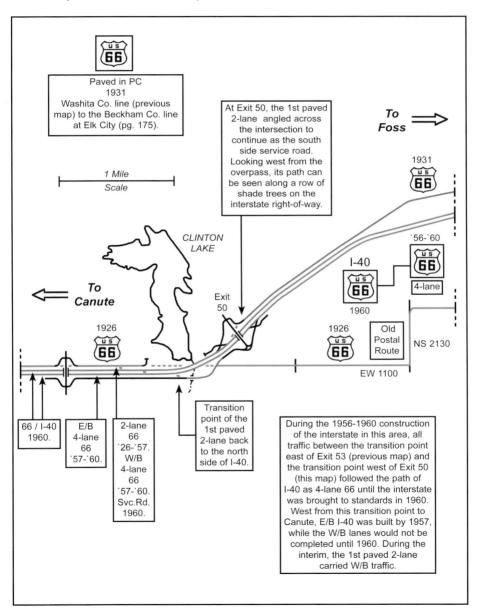

US 66

Paved in PC
1931
Washita Co. line (previous map) to the Beckham Co. line at Elk City (pg. 175).

At Exit 50, the 1st paved 2-lane angled across the intersection to continue as the south side service road. Looking west from the overpass, its path can be seen along a row of shade trees on the interstate right-of-way.

To Foss ⟹

1931
US 66

1 Mile
Scale

CLINTON LAKE

'56-'60

I-40

US 66

US 66

4-lane

To Canute ⟸

Exit 50

1960

1926
US 66

1926
US 66

Old Postal Route

NS 2130

EW 1100

| 66 / I-40 1960. | E/B 4-lane 66 '57-'60. | 2-lane 66 '26-'57. W/B 4-lane 66 '57-'60. Svc.Rd. 1960. |
|---|---|---|

Transition point of the 1st paved 2-lane back to the north side of I-40.

During the 1956-1960 construction of the interstate in this area, all traffic between the transition point east of Exit 53 (previous map) and the transition point west of Exit 50 (this map) followed the path of I-40 as 4-lane 66 until the interstate was brought to standards in 1960. West from this transition point to Canute, E/B I-40 was built by 1957, while the W/B lanes would not be completed until 1960. During the interim, the 1st paved 2-lane carried W/B traffic.

*The Cotton Boll in Canute, now a private residence, had one of the more unusual names among the route's many motels.*

The hometown of former Governor David Walters, Canute (originally known as Oak), was founded in 1899 and is named for the King of Denmark. Highlights here include a 1930s WPA-built park at the east end of town and at the west end a short strip of original 2-lane paving that connects visually with its continuation across I-40.

ENTERING **CANUTE** FROM THE I-40 OVERPASS AT EXIT 47, PROCEED TO THE INTERSECTION WITH THE HISTORIC ROUTE (HWY. 66 THROUGH TOWN) AND TURN RIGHT. TURN RIGHT AGAIN AT THE INTERSECTION 1 MILE WEST, PASS BENEATH I-40 (NO ACCESS TO THE INTERSTATE), THEN TURN LEFT ON THE SERVICE ROAD AND CONTINUE TO THE JUNCTION WITH SH 34 AT ELK CITY.

*Left:*
*Though no longer renting rooms, the Washita Motel in Canute retains its vintage sign.*

*Right:*
*This historic 2-lane remnant on the west end of Canute was discarded when the I-40 bypass severed the path of Route 66 at both ends of town.*

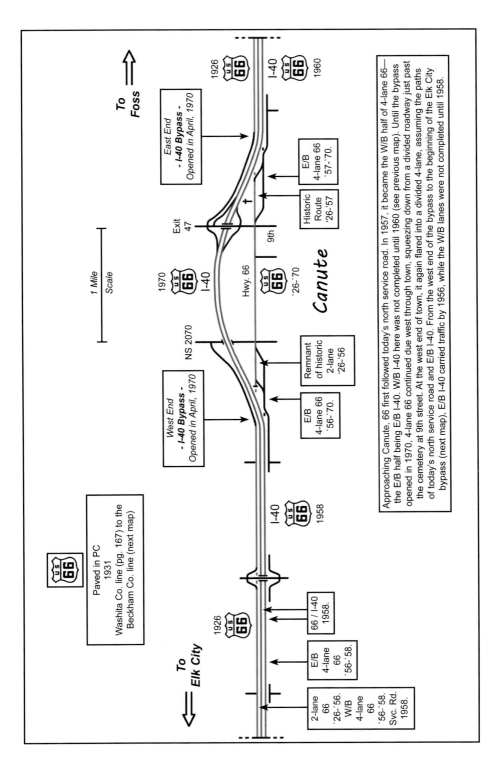

To
Foss ⟹

1926 [US 66]

I-40 [US 66] 1960

**East End - I-40 Bypass - Opened in April, 1970**

E/B 4-lane 66 '57-'70.

Historic Route '26-'57

Exit 47

9th

1 Mile
Scale

1970 [US 66] I-40

Hwy. 66

[US 66] '26-'70

*Canute*

NS 2070

**West End - I-40 Bypass - Opened in April, 1970**

Remnant of historic 2-lane '26-'56

E/B 4-lane 66 '56-'70.

I-40 [US 66] 1958

[US 66]

Paved in PC 1931 Washita Co. line (pg. 167) to the Beckham Co. line (next map)

1926 [US 66]

66 / I-40 1958.

E/B 4-lane 66 '56-'58.

To
Elk City ⟸

2-lane 66 '26-'56. W/B 4-lane 66 '56-'58. Svc. Rd. 1958.

Approaching Canute, 66 first followed today's north service road. In 1957, it became the W/B half of 4-lane 66—the E/B half being E/B I-40. W/B I-40 here was not completed until 1960 (see previous map). Until the bypass opened in 1970, 4-lane 66 continued due west through town, squeezing down from a divided roadway just past the cemetery at 9th street. At the west end of town, it again flared into a divided 4-lane, assuming the paths of today's north service road and E/B I-40. From the west end of the bypass to the beginning of the Elk City bypass (next map), E/B I-40 carried traffic by 1956, while the W/B lanes were not completed until 1958.

It is a short run westward from Canute to Elk City. And while that would seem a natural enough name for this western Oklahoma town, how the community came by that moniker is not only a story in itself, but is still considered open to discussion by some.

Back in the 1890s, two names were submitted for purposes of establishing a post office in the area. One was Crowe, the other Busch. The name Busch was the idea of one P.C. Hughes of Berlin, Oklahoma, who had thoughts of persuading the Busch company to locate a brewery there.

*A State Highway Commission 1928 date stamp in this drain just west of Elk City identifies the original lanes of the present divided 4-lane.*

*Left: Elk City's National Route 66 Museum was established in 1998. The kachina sculpture, affectionately known as Myrtle, once stood on the grounds of Queenan's Indian Trading Post at the west edge of the city.*

*Right: The eye-grabbing sign at the Elk City museum complex.*

*"The Grill" in Elk City, ca. 1948. Notice the juke box at left center of photo.*

*Postcard by Blair Cedar & Novelty Works, Camdenton, MO.*
*Laurel Kane collection*

This name became official in 1901, however it did not sit well with some folks, including Nancy Keen, who owned a boarding house near Canute. Ms. Keen was active in the Temperance Union and was otherwise a woman of some local influence. It is reported that the ensuing crusade included, among other acts, protesting attempts to paint "Busch" on the train depot. In 1907, she and her supporters won out and the town was officially named Elk City after nearby Elk Creek, which itself had been named for Indian Chief Elk River.

By 1941, Elk City had developed an innovative program that could possibly be credited with setting the stage for health insurance as it became known. Created by local physician M. Shadid, with sponsorship from The Farmers' Co-operative Hospital Association and the local hospital here, it made available, for $25.00 per year, complete medical coverage for a member and his immediate family.

---

FROM THE INTERSECTION WITH SH 34 AT **ELK CITY**, MAKE A LEFT / RIGHT JOG TO ACCESS BUS. 40 AND FOLLOW IT UNTIL IT CURVES LEFT AND BECOMES VAN BUREN, WHICH IN TURN CURVES RIGHT ONTO 3RD STREET (SEE MAPS ON PAGES 174 AND 175). CONTINUE WESTBOUND ON 3RD STREET THROUGH TOWN. WEST OF THE CITY, APPROXIMATELY 2 MILES BEYOND THE TURNOFF FOR SH 6, WATCH FOR THE CONNECTION WITH SH 34. JUST PAST THIS JUNCTION, TURN ONTO THE HISTORIC 2-LANE, WHICH HOOKS OFF TO THE RIGHT TO BECOME THE SERVICE ROAD FOR I-40.

---

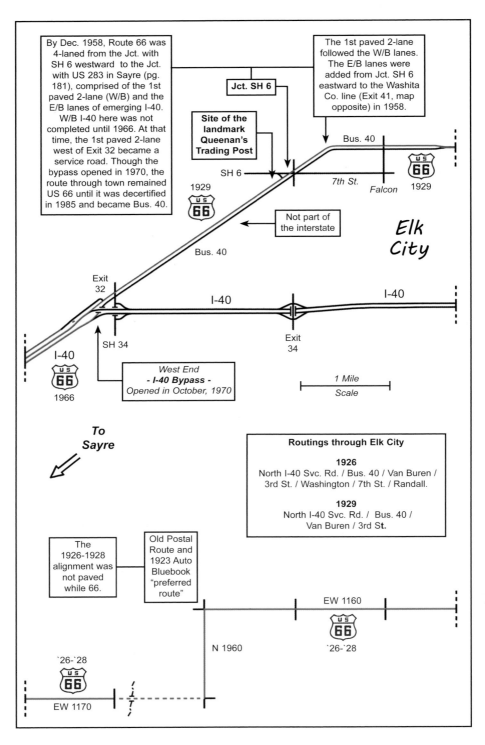

By Dec. 1958, Route 66 was 4-laned from the Jct. with SH 6 westward to the Jct. with US 283 in Sayre (pg. 181), comprised of the 1st paved 2-lane (W/B) and the E/B lanes of emerging I-40. W/B I-40 here was not completed until 1966. At that time, the 1st paved 2-lane west of Exit 32 became a service road. Though the bypass opened in 1970, the route through town remained US 66 until it was decertified in 1985 and became Bus. 40.

The 1st paved 2-lane followed the W/B lanes. The E/B lanes were added from Jct. SH 6 eastward to the Washita Co. line (Exit 41, map opposite) in 1958.

Jct. SH 6

Site of the landmark Queenan's Trading Post

Bus. 40

US 66

1929

SH 6

7th St.

Falcon

1929

1929

US 66

Not part of the interstate

Elk City

Bus. 40

Exit 32

I-40

I-40

I-40

SH 34

Exit 34

I-40

US 66

1966

West End
- I-40 Bypass -
Opened in October, 1970

1 Mile
Scale

To Sayre

Routings through Elk City

**1926**
North I-40 Svc. Rd. / Bus. 40 / Van Buren / 3rd St. / Washington / 7th St. / Randall.

**1929**
North I-40 Svc. Rd. / Bus. 40 / Van Buren / 3rd St.

The 1926-1928 alignment was not paved while 66.

Old Postal Route and 1923 Auto Bluebook "preferred route"

EW 1160

US 66

N 1960

`26-`28

`26-`28

US 66

EW 1170

EW 1170

174

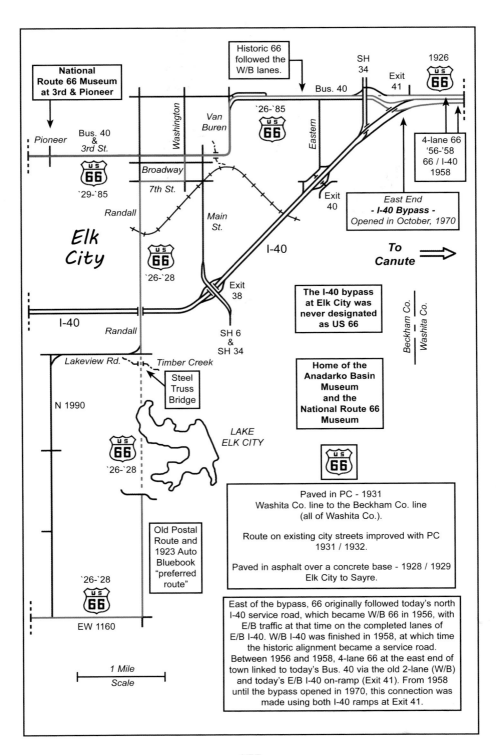

National
Route 66 Museum
at 3rd & Pioneer

Historic 66 followed the W/B lanes.

SH 34

Exit 41

1926

US 66

Bus. 40

`26-`85

US 66

Washington

Van Buren

Eastern

Pioneer

Bus. 40 & 3rd St.

US 66

`29-`85

Broadway

7th St.

4-lane 66 '56-'58
66 / I-40
1958

Randall

Main St.

Exit 40

East End
- I-40 Bypass -
Opened in October, 1970

Elk City

US 66

`26-`28

I-40

To Canute

Exit 38

The I-40 bypass at Elk City was never designated as US 66

I-40

Randall

SH 6 & SH 34

Beckham Co.

Washita Co.

Lakeview Rd.

Timber Creek

Steel Truss Bridge

Home of the
Anadarko Basin Museum
and the
National Route 66 Museum

N 1990

US 66

`26-`28

LAKE ELK CITY

US 66

Old Postal Route and 1923 Auto Bluebook "preferred route"

Paved in PC - 1931
Washita Co. line to the Beckham Co. line
(all of Washita Co.).

Route on existing city streets improved with PC
1931 / 1932.

Paved in asphalt over a concrete base - 1928 / 1929
Elk City to Sayre.

`26-`28

US 66

EW 1160

1 Mile
Scale

East of the bypass, 66 originally followed today's north I-40 service road, which became W/B 66 in 1956, with E/B traffic at that time on the completed lanes of E/B I-40. W/B I-40 was finished in 1958, at which time the historic alignment became a service road. Between 1956 and 1958, 4-lane 66 at the east end of town linked to today's Bus. 40 via the old 2-lane (W/B) and today's E/B I-40 on-ramp (Exit 41). From 1958 until the bypass opened in 1970, this connection was made using both I-40 ramps at Exit 41.

*Elm Grove Motel between Elk City and Sayre (site identified on page 179).*
*Courtesy Bill Webb*

The program was described by Jack Rittenhouse in *A Guide Book to Highway 66* as "an unusual experiment in group medical care."

Elk City was also the starting point for yet another early re-alignment of major proportions, though it did not adversely affect any communities. Initially, the highway followed the old Postal Route westward from town, as depicted on the maps. Yet only two years after the highway's dedication in 1926, what became the first paved alignment here and later the corridor of I-40 was built between Elk City and Sayre to eliminate the zigzagging historic pathway.

Today, Elk City is home to an abundance of historic architecture and many points of interests, including the Anadarko Basin Museum of Natural History at 107 E. 3rd. and the National Route 66 Museum at 3rd (Route 66) and Pioneer. Perhaps the best known landmark here, at least in terms of Route 66 history, is the former Queenan's Trading Post, which once operated on the first paved alignment just west of town at the junction with SH 6.

The trading post was built in 1948 by proprietors Reese and Wanda Queenan, who were already seasoned traders of curios and Indian wares up and down Route 66. With traffic steadily climbing toward the peak it would reach in the 1950s, business was good. Before long Queenan's became a permanent fixture on the west side of Elk City. Even so, competition was on the rise and entrepreneurs from Chicago to Los Angeles were going all out to snag more tourist dollars than the next guy. The result was a roadside soon clogged with every kind of signage and other attention-grabbing device imaginable.

To keep up with the Joneses, so to speak, the Queenans decided to erect a giant kachina in front of the trading post. This was accomplished by Reese, with help from a Sayre welder who sculpted the towering figure from oil drums and steel pipe. For good measure, they soon added a much huskier kachina, complete with a skirt.

In 1962, Reese passed away, and the trading post finally closed in 1980. Today, both of these remarkable artifacts stand in front of Elk City's National Route 66 Museum as a permanent tribute to the enterprising Queenans.

*Right:*
*Wanda and Reese Queenan inside their trading post, ca. 1955.*

*Below:*
*The tall kachina welcomes motorists to Queenan's Indian Trading Post in the mid-1950s.*
Wanda Queenan

*Above: The big kachina, known as "Myrtle," in 1962.*
Wanda Queenan

AFTER ACCESSING THE NORTH I-40 SERVICE ROAD (HISTORIC ROUTE 66) WEST OF ELK CITY, PROCEED FOR APPROXIMATELY 4 MILES TO THE T-INTERSECTION AND TURN LEFT TO CROSS OVER THE INTERSTATE. TURN RIGHT ON THE SOUTH SIDE OF I-40, CROSS THE TRUSS BRIDGE ON TIMBER CREEK, THEN CROSS BACK TO THE NORTH SIDE OF I-40 AT THE NEXT STOP SIGN AND TURN LEFT ON THE SERVICE ROAD ONCE AGAIN TO CONTINUE TOWARD SAYRE.

*The scenic and often photographed bridge on Timber Creek west of Elk City, a classic Modified Pratt through truss design built in 1928.*

Leaving Elk City, the first paved 2-lane follows the westbound half of the 4-lane until it digresses just before the entrance to I-40, where it hooks off to become the service road. Near Timber Creek, 2-lane 66 made a sweeping curve in order to conquer this terrain obstacle. I-40, on the other hand, kept its course when confronted with the creek, thereby cutting through the historic 2-lane twice within a one mile distance. As a result, the Timber Creek Bridge now sits isolated next to the interstate on what became the south I-40 service road.

The historic pathway from Elk City stayed with the old Postal Route due south from the main business district, following the section line grids all the way to Sayre. This helps explain why a realignment from Elk City to Sayre took place as early as 1928. Along the short-lived historic pathway is the tiny community of Doxey, which had a post office from 1902 until 1931.

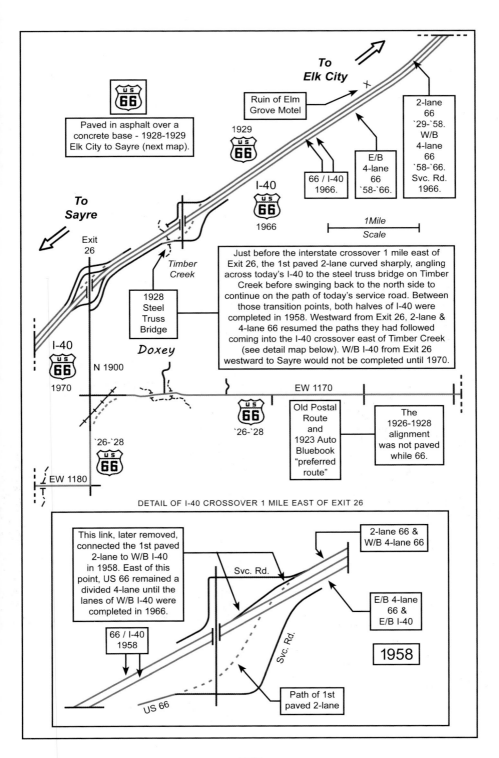

**To Elk City**

US 66

Paved in asphalt over a concrete base - 1928-1929 Elk City to Sayre (next map).

Ruin of Elm Grove Motel

1929

US 66

2-lane 66 '29-'58. W/B 4-lane 66 '58-'66. Svc. Rd. 1966.

E/B 4-lane 66 '58-'66.

66 / I-40 1966.

I-40

US 66

1966

**To Sayre**

Exit 26

Timber Creek

1928 Steel Truss Bridge

*Doxey*

I-40

US 66

1970

N 1900

'26-'28

US 66

EW 1180

1Mile
Scale

Just before the interstate crossover 1 mile east of Exit 26, the 1st paved 2-lane curved sharply, angling across today's I-40 to the steel truss bridge on Timber Creek before swinging back to the north side to continue on the path of today's service road. Between those transition points, both halves of I-40 were completed in 1958. Westward from Exit 26, 2-lane & 4-lane 66 resumed the paths they had followed coming into the I-40 crossover east of Timber Creek (see detail map below). W/B I-40 from Exit 26 westward to Sayre would not be completed until 1970.

EW 1170

US 66

'26-'28

Old Postal Route and 1923 Auto Bluebook "preferred route"

The 1926-1928 alignment was not paved while 66.

DETAIL OF I-40 CROSSOVER 1 MILE EAST OF EXIT 26

This link, later removed, connected the 1st paved 2-lane to W/B I-40 in 1958. East of this point, US 66 remained a divided 4-lane until the lanes of W/B I-40 were completed in 1966.

2-lane 66 & W/B 4-lane 66

Svc. Rd.

E/B 4-lane 66 & E/B I-40

66 / I-40 1958

Svc. Rd.

1958

US 66

Path of 1st paved 2-lane

179

*The stately Beckham County Courthouse was featured in the film adaptation of John Steinbeck's "The Grapes of Wrath."*

Sayre is the seat of Beckham County. Named for railroad investor Robert H. Sayre, it was founded in 1901 along the North Fork of the Red River. Though it may be most readily identified by its courthouse, which made an appearance in the film, *The Grapes of Wrath*, Sayre is also where former boxing champion Jess Willard once operated a boarding house, and it is the site of a century-old border dispute with Texas.

Prior to 1896, all land south of the river was claimed by the state of Texas. But in that year the US Supreme Court ruled that the river's southern fork, as opposed to the northern fork,

*This colorful mural is on the side of a tavern visible to westbound motorists entering Sayre.*

*Mural copyright Rick Anderson*

APPROACHING **SAYRE**, TURN RIGHT AT THE JUNCTION WITH BUS. 40 (EXIT 25) ONTO THE 4-LANE AND PROCEED TO THE JUNCTION WITH US 283 (4TH STREET), THEN TURN LEFT. STAY ON 4TH STREET THROUGH TOWN AND ACROSS THE NORTH FORK OF THE RED RIVER. ABOUT 1/4 OF A MILE SOUTH OF THE RIVER, WATCH FOR THE TURNOFF TO SAYRE CITY PARK. TURN RIGHT AT THE PARK, GO TO THE T-INTERSECTION, THEN TURN LEFT. CONTINUE TO THE "Y" (MAP ON PAGE 182) AND BEAR RIGHT UNTIL IT CONNECTS WITH THE SERVICE ROAD TO I-40. TURN RIGHT HERE TO CONTINUE WEST TOWARD ERICK.

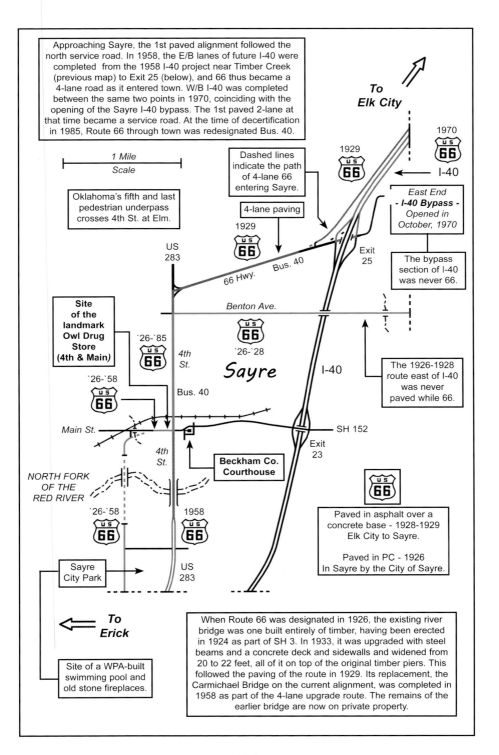

Approaching Sayre, the 1st paved alignment followed the north service road. In 1958, the E/B lanes of future I-40 were completed from the 1958 I-40 project near Timber Creek (previous map) to Exit 25 (below), and 66 thus became a 4-lane road as it entered town. W/B I-40 was completed between the same two points in 1970, coinciding with the opening of the Sayre I-40 bypass. The 1st paved 2-lane at that time became a service road. At the time of decertification in 1985, Route 66 through town was redesignated Bus. 40.

1 Mile
Scale

Oklahoma's fifth and last pedestrian underpass crosses 4th St. at Elm.

Dashed lines indicate the path of 4-lane 66 entering Sayre.

4-lane paving

1929

To
Elk City

1929

1970

I-40

East End
- I-40 Bypass -
Opened in
October, 1970

The bypass section of I-40 was never 66.

US 283

1929

66 Hwy.

Bus. 40

Exit 25

Site of the landmark Owl Drug Store (4th & Main)

Benton Ave.

'26-'85

'26-'28

4th St.

Sayre

I-40

The 1926-1928 route east of I-40 was never paved while 66.

'26-'58

Bus. 40

Main St.

4th St.

Exit 23

SH 152

NORTH FORK OF THE RED RIVER

Beckham Co. Courthouse

'26-'58

1958

Sayre City Park

US 283

Paved in asphalt over a concrete base - 1928-1929 Elk City to Sayre.

Paved in PC - 1926 In Sayre by the City of Sayre.

To Erick

Site of a WPA-built swimming pool and old stone fireplaces.

When Route 66 was designated in 1926, the existing river bridge was one built entirely of timber, having been erected in 1924 as part of SH 3. In 1933, it was upgraded with steel beams and a concrete deck and sidewalls and widened from 20 to 22 feet, all of it on top of the original timber piers. This followed the paving of the route in 1929. Its replacement, the Carmichael Bridge on the current alignment, was completed in 1958 as part of the 4-lane upgrade route. The remains of the earlier bridge are now on private property.

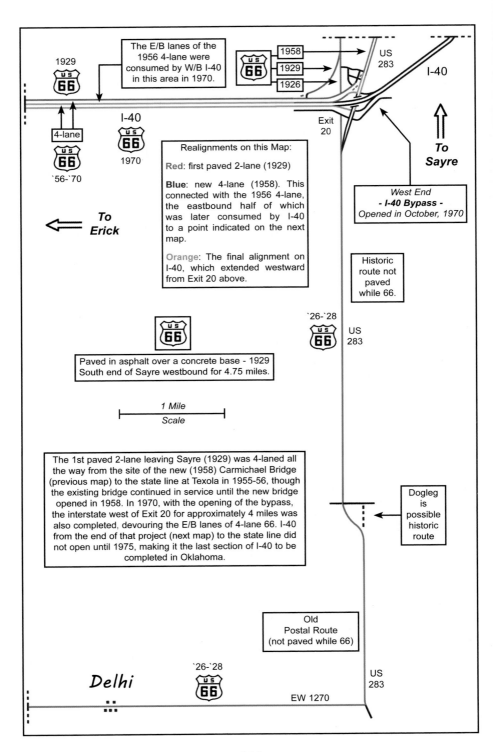

**1929**
US 66

The E/B lanes of the 1956 4-lane were consumed by W/B I-40 in this area in 1970.

US 66
1958
1929
1926

US 283

I-40

I-40
US 66

Exit 20

4-lane
US 66
`56-`70

US 66
1970

**To Sayre**

**Realignments on this Map:**

Red: first paved 2-lane (1929)

Blue: new 4-lane (1958). This connected with the 1956 4-lane, the eastbound half of which was later consumed by I-40 to a point indicated on the next map.

Orange: The final alignment on I-40, which extended westward from Exit 20 above.

**To Erick**

West End
- *I-40 Bypass* -
Opened in October, 1970

Historic route not paved while 66.

`26-`28

US 66

US 283

US 66

Paved in asphalt over a concrete base - 1929
South end of Sayre westbound for 4.75 miles.

1 Mile
Scale

The 1st paved 2-lane leaving Sayre (1929) was 4-laned all the way from the site of the new (1958) Carmichael Bridge (previous map) to the state line at Texola in 1955-56, though the existing bridge continued in service until the new bridge opened in 1958. In 1970, with the opening of the bypass, the interstate west of Exit 20 for approximately 4 miles was also completed, devouring the E/B lanes of 4-lane 66. I-40 from the end of that project (next map) to the state line did not open until 1975, making it the last section of I-40 to be completed in Oklahoma.

Dogleg is possible historic route

Old
Postal Route
(not paved while 66)

*Delhi*

`26-`28
US 66

EW 1270

US 283

*Looking east on Sayre's Main Street toward the Beckham County Courthouse, ca. 1965.*

Baxter Lane, Amarillo, TX. Steve Rider collection

defined the true boundary between the two states. As a result, the area between the Red River's north and south forks became part of Oklahoma Territory. In 1924, when SH 3 was designated along the path of the Postal Route, a timber bridge was built on the river here (shown on the map on page 181 and pictured below). The bridge on today's 4-lane alignment opened in 1958. What remains of its 1924 predecessor, once part of the historic alignment following Main westward from 4th Street, is now on private property (see map).

*Construction of the timber bridge at Sayre in 1924.*
*Oklahoma Department of Transportation - Annual Report for 1928.*

Crossing the North Fork of the Red River at Sayre, Beckham County, Oklahoma. This bridge contains 456,000 feet of lumber, 14,000 lineal feet of creosoted piles, 2,600 feet long exclusive of 200 feet of dirt approaches and was constructed by The Mann Construction Co., highway construction contractors, of Oklahoma City, at a contract price of $63,971.60. It is on State Highway No. 3.

*Left:*
*Remains of the modified 1924 timber bridge at Sayre.*

*Below:*
*Entrance to the WPA rock swimming pool in Sayre City Park.*
Kathy Anderson

In addition to the county courthouse, Sayre is home to the Short Grass Country Museum and Historical Society, located in the old Rock Island train depot. Other landmarks include the Owl Drug at 4th and Main Streets and the old hotel on Main just a block to the west on the historic alignment. 14 Flags Sayre City Park, on the south side of the river, is bordered on the east by the upgrade alignment of Route 66 and on the west by the historic route, where fire pits and a rock swimming pool built by the WPA still stand.

South of the park, the historic route continued on the path of the old Postal Route all the way to Texola by way of Delhi (founded in 1893 and named for the capital of India).

Also south of the park, both the 1929 and the upgrade route turned west to follow along the railroad tracks toward Erick by way of the tiny farming community of Hext, named in 1901 for local resident William Hext, (map opposite).

This stretch was 4-laned

*Hext, now sandwiched between former 4-lane 66 and I-40.*

STAY WITH THE I-40 SERVICE ROAD WEST FROM SAYRE (WHICH BECOMES PART OF A FORMER DIVIDED 4-LANE AFTER 4 MILES) THROUGH **HEXT** TO ERICK.

Paved in asphalt over a concrete base - 1929
From Sayre W/B for 4.75 miles (includes the 1st mile on this map).

Paved in PC - 1929
From the end of above project W/B for 2.8 miles (approx. 1 mile west of Hext).

Paved in PC - 1930 - From 1 mile west of Hext to Erick (next map).

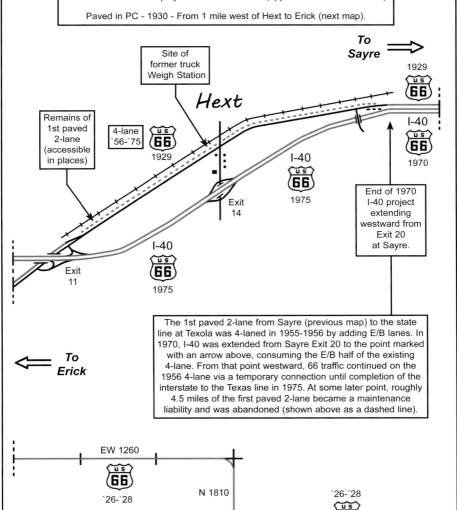

To Sayre

1929

Site of former truck Weigh Station

*Hext*

Remains of 1st paved 2-lane (accessible in places)

4-lane `56-`75

U S 66
1929

I-40

U S 66
1970

I-40

U S 66
1975

Exit 14

End of 1970 I-40 project extending westward from Exit 20 at Sayre.

I-40

U S 66
1975

Exit 11

The 1st paved 2-lane from Sayre (previous map) to the state line at Texola was 4-laned in 1955-1956 by adding E/B lanes. In 1970, I-40 was extended from Sayre Exit 20 to the point marked with an arrow above, consuming the E/B half of the existing 4-lane. From that point westward, 66 traffic continued on the 1956 4-lane via a temporary connection until completion of the interstate to the Texas line in 1975. At some later point, roughly 4.5 miles of the first paved 2-lane became a maintenance liability and was abandoned (shown above as a dashed line).

To Erick

EW 1260

U S 66
`26-`28

N 1810

EW 1270

`26-`28

U S 66

Old Postal Route (not paved while 66)

1 Mile
Scale

*Erick's 100th Meridian Museum.*
*Just the name draws visitors.*

in the mid-1950s, and was the last section of Oklahoma road to lose its US 66 designation to I-40. The westbound lanes (the first paved 2-lane alignment), which are on a less favorable grade than the added eastbound lanes in this area, were ultimately abandoned to reduce ongoing maintenance costs.

Named for Beeks Erick, who developed the town for the Choctaw Town Site and Improvement Company, Erick was founded in 1901 as a farming community, with natural gas figuring in prominently a few years later. Erick is the home of singers "King of the Road" Roger Miller and "Purple People Eater" Sheb Wooley. At the crossroads named for these two icons, two of the buildings house the 100th Meridian Museum and the Roger Miller Museum. A block south is the historic Sand Hills Curiosity Shop in the old City Meat Market Building, and leaving town on the old road, a couple of deteriorating motels (the West Winds and the Elm) barely hang on.

FROM **ERICK**, CONTINUE ON THE OLD 4-LANE TO **TEXOLA** AND THE TEXAS STATE LINE.

*Erick's old City Meat Market is now home to the Sandhills Curiosity Shop.*

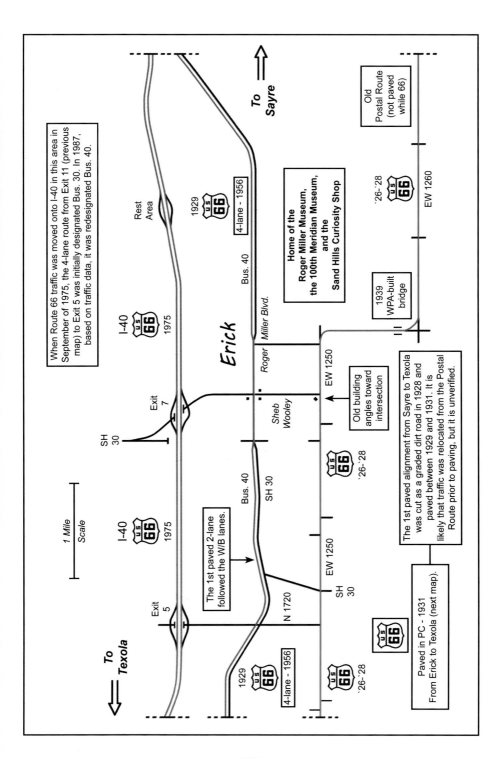

When Route 66 traffic was moved onto I-40 in this area in September of 1975, the 4-lane route from Exit 11 (previous map) to Exit 5 was initially designated Bus. 30. In 1987, based on traffic data, it was redesignated Bus. 40.

To Sayre

Rest Area

1929 US 66

4-lane - 1956

Bus. 40

Roger Miller Blvd.

Erick

I-40 US 66 1975

Exit 7

SH 30

Home of the
**Roger Miller Museum,
the 100th Meridian Museum,
and the
Sand Hills Curiosity Shop**

Old Postal Route (not paved while 66)

'26-'28 US 66

EW 1260

1939 WPA-built bridge

EW 1250

Old building angles toward intersection

Sheb Wooley

'26-'28 US 66

SH 30

Bus. 40

The 1st paved alignment from Sayre to Texola was cut as a graded dirt road in 1928 and paved between 1929 and 1931. It is likely that traffic was relocated from the Postal Route prior to paving, but it is unverified.

The 1st paved 2-lane followed the W/B lanes.

1 Mile Scale

I-40 US 66 1975

Exit 5

EW 1250

SH 30

N 1720

To Texola

1929 US 66

4-lane - 1956

'26-'28 US 66

Paved in PC - 1931
From Erick to Texola (next map).

US 66

Texola is often referred to as a ghost town, though the scattering of folks entrenched here who still call Texola home might argue that charge. In any case, the little town on the Texas border established its post office in 1901. It has been formerly known as both Texoma and Texokla, and the 1910 Territorial Jail still stands as a symbolic warning to would-be lawbreakers. In *A Guide Book to Highway 66*, author Jack Rittenhouse described Texola in 1946 as a town with "an old section of stores which truly savor of pioneer days. They have sidewalk awnings of wood and metal, supported by posts. Old timers still lounge on the corners."

*Texola's Water Hole No. 2 may have gone dry, but these Jack Russell Terrier pups were still on duty.*

And so it is here our journey across Oklahoma comes to a close. The awnings are long gone, as are the loitering old timers, but Texola, not unlike Quapaw, continues to pulse with the spirit of Route 66, and in that sense, its presence is as potent as ever.

*Left: Abandoned house near downtown Texola.*

*Right: A few shuttered buildings are all that remain of Texola's business district.*

*Below:*
*Prisoner's perspective from the one room jail at Texola.*

*Above:*
*Texola's Territorial Jail—secure lodging for early 20th century bandits.*

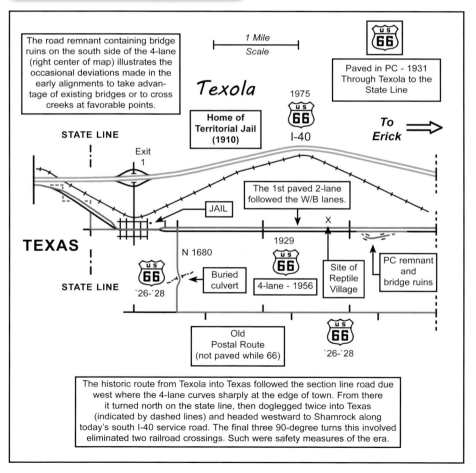

The road remnant containing bridge ruins on the south side of the 4-lane (right center of map) illustrates the occasional deviations made in the early alignments to take advantage of existing bridges or to cross creeks at favorable points.

1 Mile
Scale

**US 66**

Paved in PC - 1931 Through Texola to the State Line

*Texola*

1975

**US 66**

I-40

**To Erick** ⟹

STATE LINE

Exit 1

**Home of Territorial Jail (1910)**

JAIL

The 1st paved 2-lane followed the W/B lanes.

X

**TEXAS**

N 1680

1929

**US 66**

Site of Reptile Village

PC remnant and bridge ruins

STATE LINE

**US 66**

'26-'28

Buried culvert

4-lane - 1956

Old Postal Route (not paved while 66)

**US 66**

'26-'28

The historic route from Texola into Texas followed the section line road due west where the 4-lane curves sharply at the edge of town. From there it turned north on the state line, then doglegged twice into Texas (indicated by dashed lines) and headed westward to Shamrock along today's south I-40 service road. The final three 90-degree turns this involved eliminated two railroad crossings. Such were safety measures of the era.

*Following the decertification of US 66 in 1985, its signs
were removed and sold at special auctions conducted by ODOT.*

# Afterword

We began our quest of Oklahoma US 66 at the Kansas state line near Quapaw and switched the ignition off at Texola. Those who have actually made that journey know that the 400 miles of Mother Road reflected in the rearview mirror promise a return trip as memorable as the one just taken. Many of them also know that venturing beyond the established pathway to discover the highway's roots, one layer at a time, is where the true adventure lies.

Anyone taking to the road with *Oklahoma Route 66* will, in the least, be introduced to its many alignments. They may also be treated to the excitement that comes from connecting with some of its reaches for the first time, or meeting a few of the highway's keepers, or perhaps just for a while getting lost in time. Possibly, one outing will inspire another. If any of these things take place, then this book will have served its purpose.

Oklahoma Route 66. It is a road paved with history and delightfully diverse. You can hop on it anywhere you like for a casual cruise, or pack a suitcase and not come back until every page between these covers is dirt-stained and dog-eared. So give it a try. Highway guardians like Cy Avery, Will Rogers, Andy Payne, and "Mr. 66" himself—Jack Cutberth, would heartily recommend it.

# Eastbound Driving Directions

FROM THE TEXAS STATE LINE PROCEED ON THE 4-LANE THROUGH **TEXOLA**, **ERICK**, AND **HEXT** TOWARD SAYRE.

APPROACHING EXIT 20 AT SAYRE, THE ROAD CURVES LEFT ALONGSIDE I-40, ENDING AT A STOP SIGN WITH THE 4-LANE (US 283). TURN LEFT AND TAKE THE 4-LANE ACROSS THE NORTH FORK OF THE RED RIVER INTO **SAYRE**,
OR,
FOR THE EARLY ROUTE, TURN LEFT BEFORE THE I-40 INTERCHANGE (SEE MAP ON PG. 183), THEN RIGHT AT THE NORTH END OF SAYRE CITY PARK, THEN LEFT AGAIN ONTO THE 4-LANE, ACROSS THE RIVER, AND INTO SAYRE.

TAKE US 283 (4TH STREET) THROUGH SAYRE, TURN RIGHT ON BUS. 40 (66 HWY.), THEN TURN LEFT ONTO THE I-40 SERVICE ROAD JUST _BEFORE_ EXIT 25.

AT THE NEXT INTERSECTION (EXIT 26), CROSS TO THE SOUTH SIDE OF I-40, TURN LEFT ON THE SERVICE ROAD, CROSS TIMBER CREEK, THEN CROSS BACK TO THE NORTH SIDE OF THE INTERSTATE AT THE NEXT OPPORTUNITY, TURNING RIGHT TO RESUME ON THE SERVICE ROAD TOWARD ELK CITY.

WHERE THE SERVICE ROAD INTERSECTS THE DIVIDED 4-LANE (EXIT 32), TURN LEFT TO CONTINUE, ENTERING **ELK CITY** ON BUS. 40/3RD STREET. FOLLOW 3RD UNTIL IT CURVES LEFT ONTO VAN BUREN AND THEN CURVES RIGHT TO CONTINUE EAST ON BUS. 40. AT THE INTERSECTION WITH SH 34, TURN LEFT, THEN IMMEDIATELY RIGHT TO ACCESS THE NORTH I-40 SERVICE ROAD.

STAY WITH THE NORTH SERVICE ROAD ALL THE WAY TO THE T-INTERSECTION NEAR **CANUTE.** TURN RIGHT HERE, PASS BENEATH I-40, THEN TURN LEFT TO ENTER TOWN. AFTER ONE MILE, TURN LEFT AT THE INTERSECTION WITH 9TH STREET, CROSS OVER I-40, AND TURN RIGHT ON THE NORTH SERVICE ROAD.

CROSS BACK OVER I-40 AT THE FIRST CHANCE, TURN LEFT ON THE SERVICE ROAD, THEN CROSS BACK TO THE NORTH SIDE OF THE INTERSTATE AT THE NEXT OPPORTUNITY (EXIT 50) AND TURN RIGHT.

AT THE STOP SIGN AT SH 44 AT **FOSS**, CONTINUE EASTWARD THROUGH THE INTERSECTION TO THE NEXT CROSSOVER POINT (EXIT 57), TURN RIGHT, PASS BENEATH I-40, THEN TURN LEFT ON THE SOUTH SERVICE ROAD TO CONTINUE.

FOLLOW THE SERVICE ROAD DUE EAST ALL THE WAY TO **CLINTON**, CURVING LEFT AT NEPTUNE PARK, THEN ENTERING TOWN AFTER PASSING UNDER I-40. NOW ON 10TH STREET, FOLLOW IT TO FRISCO, TURN RIGHT, STAY WITH FRISCO TO 4TH STREET, TURN LEFT, THEN TURN RIGHT ON GARY BLVD.,
OR,

FOR A LATER ROUTING, TURN RIGHT FROM 10TH ONTO OPAL, THEN LEFT ONTO 4TH AND RIGHT AGAIN AT GARY BLVD.,
OR,
FOR THE FINAL ROUTING, TAKE 10TH TO GARY, TURN LEFT AND FOLLOW IT WESTBOUND, THEN TURN AROUND AFTER PASSING THE ROUTE 66 MUSEUM AND STAY WITH GARY BLVD. EASTBOUND ALL THE WAY THROUGH TOWN.

AFTER CROSSING THE WASHITA RIVER ON GARY BLVD., ACCESS THE OLD 2-LANE <u>BEFORE</u> THE I-40 OVERPASS (EXIT 69) BY JOGGING LEFT AND THEN RIGHT. PROCEED EASTBOUND ON THE SERVICE ROAD AND CROSS OVER I-40 AT THE FIRST CHANCE (ABOUT 1 MILE), THEN TURN LEFT TO CONTINUE.

STAY WITH THE SOUTH SERVICE ROAD EASTBOUND PAST I-40 EXIT 71, THEN CROSS TO THE NORTH SIDE AT THE NEXT CROSSROAD AND TURN RIGHT ON THE SERVICE ROAD TO CONTINUE TOWARD WEATHERFORD.

PROCEED EASTBOUND ON THE NORTH SERVICE ROAD ALL THE WAY TO **WEATHERFORD**, FOLLOWING THE CURVE LEFT ONTO 4TH STREET TO MAIN. TURN RIGHT ON MAIN AND CONTINUE THROUGH TOWN. AT WASHINGTON, TURN LEFT, THEN IMMEDIATELY RIGHT TO PARALLEL I-40 ON EAST MAIN STREET TO THE STOP SIGN (EAST DAVIS / EAST MAIN). TURN RIGHT HERE TO CONTINUE.

STAY WITH THE NORTH SERVICE ROAD THROUGH **HYDRO** AND CONTINUE EASTWARD ALL THE WAY PAST **BRIDGEPORT** AND THE HINTON JUNCTION (US 281) TO THE **PONY BRIDGE** ON THE SOUTH CANADIAN RIVER.

TO FOLLOW THE 1ST PAVED ALIGNMENT EAST OF THE PONY BRIDGE, TAKE THE FIRST RIGHT BEYOND THE BRIDGE, ASCEND BRIDGEPORT HILL TO THE JCT. WITH US 281 SPUR, TURN RIGHT ONTO THE 4-LANE, THEN TURN LEFT ONTO THE OLD 2-LANE JUST BEFORE THE JCT. WITH I-40 AT EXIT 108. PROCEED EAST TO THE STOP SIGN AT US 270 (SOUTH OF CALUMET), THEN CONTINUE EAST TOWARD EL RENO.
OR,
FOR THE HISTORIC ROUTE, FROM THE EAST SIDE OF THE PONY BRIDGE, STAY WITH US 281 NORTHERLY TO THE JCT. WITH US 281 SPUR, TURN LEFT, PROCEED TO **GEARY**, TURN RIGHT ON US 270, AND TAKE US 270 TO **CALUMET** AND ONWARD TO THE STOP SIGN 4 MILES SOUTH OF CALUMET. TURN LEFT HERE AND CONTINUE TOWARD EL RENO.

WHERE THE 2-LANE JUNCTIONS WITH THE 4-LANE NEAR THE ENTRANCE TO FORT RENO, TURN LEFT AND TAKE THE 4-LANE (BUS. 40) INTO **EL RENO,** ENTERING ON SUNSET BLVD. AT CHOCTAW, TURN RIGHT ONE BLOCK, THEN LEFT ON WADE FOR TWO BLOCKS, CROSSING ROCK ISLAND TO A RIGHT ON HOFF, THEN A LEFT AT ELM, A RIGHT ON SHEPARD, THEN A LEFT ONTO SH 66,
OR,
WHEN WADE INTERSECTS ROCK ISLAND, TURN RIGHT AND FOLLOW ROCK ISLAND ONTO SH 66 AND CONTINUE TOWARD YUKON.
STAY WITH SH 66 PAST **BANNER** TO **YUKON**, AND CRUISE STRAIGHT THROUGH TOWN ON MAIN. ON THE EAST SIDE OF YUKON, CONTINUE ON THE 4-LANE FROM THE INTERSECTION WITH MUSTANG ROAD TOWARD BETHANY,

OR,

JUST PAST THE INTERSECTION WITH MUSTANG ROAD HOOK RIGHT ONTO THE HISTORIC 2-LANE, FOLLOW IT EAST TO THE "Y" AT LAKE OVERHOLSER, BEAR LEFT, THEN TRACK ALONG THE NORTH SHORE OF THE LAKE TOWARD THE OLD OVERHOLSER BRIDGE. JUST BEFORE THE BRIDGE (CLOSED), TURN LEFT TO CONNECT WITH THE 4-LANE, THEN RIGHT INTO **BETHANY**, NOW ON 39TH EXP.

STAY WITH 39TH EXP. THROUGH BETHANY AND **WARR ACRES** INTO OKLAHOMA CITY.

FOR THE HISTORIC ROUTE THROUGH **OKLAHOMA CITY**: JUST EAST OF THE INTERSECTION WITH PORTLAND, 39TH EXP. DUMPS ONTO I-44. STAY EAST TO THE FIRST EXIT (MAY AVE. - JUST BEYOND THE INTERCHANGE) AND EXIT RIGHT. CONTINUE EAST THROUGH THE OFF-RAMP LIGHT AT MAY AVE. AND PROCEED ON 39TH STREET TO CLASSEN. TURN RIGHT ON CLASSEN, LEFT AT 23RD, THEN CLOVER LEAF UP ONTO LINCOLN BLVD. NORTHBOUND AFTER PASSING THROUGH THE TUNNEL UNDER THE STATE CAPITOL COMPLEX. FOLLOW LINCOLN NORTH TO I-44, TAKING THE EASTBOUND ON-RAMP. ONCE ON I-44, REMAIN IN THE RIGHT LANE AND EXIT IMMEDIATELY AT KELLEY AVE., TURNING LEFT ONTO KELLEY FROM THE OFF-RAMP,
OR,
FOR THE UPGRADE ALIGNMENT THROUGH OKLAHOMA CITY, FOLLOW THE DIRECTIONS ABOVE TO THE MAY AVE. OFF-RAMP, TURN RIGHT ONTO MAY AVE., PROCEED TO 23RD STREET, THEN TURN LEFT ON 23RD TO LINCOLN BLVD. AT THE CAPITOL COMPLEX, AND CONTINUE AS DESCRIBED ABOVE.

FROM THE JUNCTION OF I-44 AND KELLEY, PROCEED NORTH ON KELLEY TO MEMORIAL ROAD, TURN RIGHT, THEN IMMEDIATELY LEFT ONTO THE SERVICE RD. TO ACCESS BROADWAY. FOLLOW BROADWAY INTO **EDMOND** TO 2ND ST.

APPROACHING 2ND STREET, MOVE TO THE RIGHT LANE, TURN RIGHT ONTO 2ND, AND CONTINUE EAST THROUGH EDMOND AND ACROSS I-35 ONTO SH 66. STAY WITH SH 66 THROUGH **ARCADIA** AND **LUTHER**.

NEARING **WELLSTON**, BEAR LEFT ONTO SH 66B TO TAKE THE HISTORIC ROUTE THROUGH TOWN, WHICH RECONNECTS WITH SH 66,
OR,
STAY WITH SH 66 EASTBOUND PAST WELLSTON AND THROUGH **WARWICK** TO CHANDLER.

ENTERING **CHANDLER**, SWING LEFT ONTO MANVEL AVE. AND PROCEED THROUGH TOWN, FOLLOWING THE SIGNS FOR SH 66 AS IT CURVES RIGHT NEAR 5TH STREET ONTO E. 1ST STREET.

CONTINUE EASTBOUND ON SH 66 THROUGH **DAVENPORT**, **STROUD**, AND **DEPEW** TO **BRISTOW**, ENTERING TOWN ON ROLAND. CURVE RIGHT ONTO 4TH STREET, THEN TURN LEFT AT MAIN AND PROCEED EASTWARD, STILL ON SH 66.
LEAVING BRISTOW, PASS UNDER THE TURNPIKE, THEN WATCH FOR A LEFT TURN ONTO SH 48 NORTH. TURN HERE ONTO THE HISTORIC ROUTE FOR ONE MILE TO **BELLVUE**, TURN RIGHT, THEN RECONNECT WITH SH 66 AFTER ONE

MORE MILE,
OR,
STAY WITH SH 66 EASTBOUND.

ABOUT 2 1/4 MILES BEYOND THE BELLVUE LOOP, THE HISTORIC ROUTE ANGLES
OFF TO THE LEFT ONTO WHAT IS KNOWN AS THE "TANK FARM LOOP." THIS CAN
BE DRIVEN UNTIL IT REJOINS SH 66,
OR,
STAY WITH SH 66 EASTBOUND.

PROCEED THROUGH **KELLYVILLE** TOWARD SAPULPA. JUST PAST THE JCT. WITH
SH 33 (THE ROAD FLARES TO 4 LANES HERE), THE HISTORIC ROUTE ONCE
AGAIN DIGRESSES FROM THE CURRENT ALIGNMENT. TURN LEFT HERE TO
ACCESS THIS STRETCH OF ORIGINAL ROADWAY FOR 3 MILES UNTIL IT
RECONNECTS WITH SH 66 JUST PAST THE ROCK CREEK BRIDGE, THEN TURN
LEFT TO ENTER **SAPULPA**,
OR,
STAY WITH SH 66.

ENTER SAPULPA ON DEWEY, TURN LEFT AT MISSION, AND, FOR THE HISTORIC
ROUTE TO TULSA, TURN LEFT AGAIN AT THE JUNCTION FOR SH 166
(FRANKOMA ROAD / OLD SAPULPA ROAD), THEN AVOID THE TURNOFF
FOR 166 AND CONTINUE THROUGH **BOWDEN** AND **OAKHURST** AS THE ROAD
BECOMES SOUTHWEST BLVD. THROUGH **RED FORK** AND INTO **TULSA**,
OR,
STAY WITH SH 66 LEAVING SAPULPA UNTIL IT ENTERS ONTO I-44, THEN EXIT
IMMEDIATELY TO THE RIGHT AT EXIT 222A (S. 49TH W. AVENUE). AT THE
OFF-RAMP TRAFFIC SIGNAL, TURN LEFT, PASS UNDER I-44, AND CONTINUE TO
THE T-INTERSECTION AT SOUTHWEST BLVD. TURN RIGHT HERE ONTO THE
HISTORIC 2-LANE THROUGH RED FORK AND INTO TULSA.

STAY WITH SOUTHWEST BLVD. AS IT PARALLELS I-244, CROSS THE ARKANSAS
RIVER, TURN RIGHT ONTO 12TH STREET (SECOND TURN AFTER THE BRIDGE),
AND CONTINUE ON 12TH UNTIL IT ANGLES ACROSS I-444 AND CURVES RIGHT
ONTO 11TH STREET. AT BOULDER, 11TH CHANGES INTO 10TH, THEN BECOMES
11TH ONCE AGAIN AS IT ANGLES TO THE RIGHT AT THE INTERSECTION WITH
ELGIN. STAY WITH 11TH STREET ALL THE WAY TO 193RD, THEN TURN LEFT AND
PROCEED TOWARD CATOOSA.

(NOTE: FROM 11TH ST. JUST EAST OF I-444, THE HISTORIC ROUTE FOLLOWED
CHEYENNE, 7TH, DETROIT, 2ND, LEWIS, ADMIRAL PLACE, MINGO ROAD, 11TH,
AND 193RD ST. THIS ALIGNMENT CAN BE FOLLOWED USING THE MAPS.)

FROM 11TH AND 193RD PROCEED NORTH ON 193RD, PASS BENEATH I-44, THEN
TURN RIGHT ONTO CHEROKEE TO ENTER **CATOOSA**. FOLLOW CHEROKEE
THROUGH TOWN, TURNING RIGHT ONTO FORD TO CONNECT WITH 4-LANE
SH 66 AND TURN LEFT THERE TO CONTINUE.
NOTE: SH 66 IN CATOOSA CANNOT BE ACCESSED  EASTBOUND VIA I-44 FROM
193RD STREET.

FROM CATOOSA, STAY WITH SH 66 THROUGH **VERDIGRIS**, **CLAREMORE**, AND **SEQUOYAH** TO FOYIL.

JUST BEFORE **FOYIL** (ABOUT 6 MILES EAST OF SEQUOYAH) WATCH FOR A TURN TO THE RIGHT (EASY TO MISS) ONTO THE ORIGINAL 2-LANE AND FOLLOW IT THROUGH TOWN TO A RECONNECTION WITH THE 4-LANE AT SH 28A, OR, STAY WITH SH 66.

FROM FOYIL, CONTINUE ON SH 66 THROUGH **BUSHYHEAD** TO CHELSEA. TO TAKE THE HISTORIC ROUTE HERE, TURN RIGHT ON 6TH, LEFT ON CHERRY, AND RIGHT ON E. 1ST STREET TO A RECONNECTION WITH SH 66 JUST PAST THE 1926 STEEL TRUSS BRIDGE ON PRYOR CREEK, OR, STAY WITH SH 66.

FROM CHELSEA, SH 66 PASSES THROUGH **WHITE OAK**, THEN BECOMES US 60 & US 69 INTO VINITA. ENTER **VINITA** ON WILSON, TURN RIGHT ON ILLINOIS, THEN CONTINUE THROUGH TOWN AND PROCEED TO **AFTON**.

JUST EAST OF AFTON, ABOUT A HALF-MILE PAST THE HORSE CREEK BRIDGE, TURN LEFT TO TAKE THE HISTORIC ROUTE ALONG THE "SIDEWALK" HIGHWAY, FOLLOWING IT AS IT PASSES OVER I-44. AT THE NEXT INTERSECTION TURN RIGHT, THEN LEFT WHERE IT JUNCTIONS WITH THE CURRENT ROUTE, OR, STAY WITH US 60 & US 69.

1 MILE PAST **NARCISSA**, TAKE THE HISTORIC ROUTE ("SIDEWALK HIGHWAY") ONCE AGAIN BY TURNING RIGHT FOR 1 MILE, THEN LEFT FOR 1 MILE, THEN RIGHT FOR 1 1/2 MILES, THEN LEFT ONTO MIAMI'S "E" STREET S.W. PROCEED ON "E" STREET S.W. AS IT CROSSES THE NEOSHO RIVER AND BECOMES SOUTH MAIN STREET TO STEVE OWENS BLVD. IN MIAMI, OR, STAY WITH THE CURRENT ROUTE (NOW US 59 & US 69) INTO **MIAMI** (NOW ON STEVE OWENS BLVD.) TO THE INTERSECTION WITH MAIN STREET.

FROM THE INTERSECTION OF STEVE OWENS AND MAIN ST. IN MIAMI, PROCEED NORTH AND CONTINUE TO THE "Y" JUST SOUTH OF **COMMERCE**. FOR THE HISTORIC ROUTE, GO STRAIGHT AT THE "Y" ONTO MAIN STREET, TURN RIGHT ON COMMERCE STREET, THEN LEFT AGAIN AT THE JUNCTION WITH THE CURRENT ROUTE, OR, BEAR RIGHT AT THE "Y," STAYING WITH US 69, WHICH IS MICKEY MANTLE BLVD.

PROCEED EASTBOUND ON US 69 AS IT BECOMES US 69 ALT. THROUGH **QUAPAW** TO THE KANSAS STATE LINE.

# Recommended Reading

*Route 66 Sightings*, Jerry McClanahan, Jim Ross, Shellee Graham, Ghost Town Press, 2011.

*The Grapes of Wrath*, John Steinbeck, Viking Press, 1939.

*Route 66 Crossings: Historic Bridges of the Mother Road*, Jim Ross, University of Oklahoma Press, 2016.

*Route 66, The Mother Road*, Michael Wallis, St. Martin's Press, 1990; 2001.

*The Harvest Gypsies*, John Steinbeck, Copyright 1936 by *The San Francisco News*, Heyday Books, Berkeley, 1988.

*Tales From the Coral Court, Photos and Stories from a Lost Route 66 Landmark*, Shellee Graham, Virginia Publishing, 2000.

*Far From Main Street: Three Photographers in Depression-Era New Mexico*, Museum of New Mexico, Press, 1994.

*Route 66: Iconography of the American Highway*, Arthur Krim, Johns Hopkins University Press, 2003.

*Here It Is! The Route 66 Map Series*, Jim Ross and Jerry McClanahan, Ghost Town Press, 1994-2011.

*EZ66 Guide for Travelers*, Jerry McClanahan, National Historic Route 66 Federation, 2008.

*Bunion Derby*, Charles B. Kastner, University of New Mexico Press, 2007.

*Route 66, The Romance of the West*, Thomas Arthur Repp, Mock Turtle Press, 2002.

*Route 66 Lost & Found*, Russell Olsen, Voyageur Press, 2006.

*Legendary Route 66: A Journey Through Time*, Michael Karl Witzel and Gyvel Young-Witzel, Voyageur Press, 2007.

*Americana the Beautiful: Mid-Century culture in Kodachrome*, Charles Phoenix, Angel City Press, 2006.

*Teardrops and Tiny Trailers*, Douglas Heister, Gibbs Smith, 2008.

*Roadside Relics: America's Abandoned Automobiles*, Will Shiers, Motorbooks, 2006.

*The Oklahoma Route 66 Association Trip Guide*, Oklahoma Route 66 Association, published annually.

## Primary Resources

Oklahoma Department of Transportation, Oklahoma City.
Archives & Manuscripts Division, Oklahoma Historical Society,
    Oklahoma City.
*Oklahoma Place Names*, George Shirk, 2nd Edition,
    University of Oklahoma Press, 1974.
Federal Highway Administration, Washington, D.C.
*Oklahoma, A Guide to the Sooner State*, University of Oklahoma Press,
    Norman, 1941.
*A Guide Book to Highway 66*, (A facsimile of the 1946 First Edition),
    Jack Rittenhouse, University of New Mexico Press, 1989.

## About the Author

Jim Ross is a writer, photographer, and Route 66 historian whose work has appeared in a variety of books and periodicals over the past two decades. He lives on old 66 near Arcadia, Oklahoma. To learn more of his involvement with the Mother Road, visit:

www.ghost-town-press.com

# Notes